Dynamic Diplomacy
&
Foreign Policy

#TransformingIndia

Dynamic Diplomacy & Foreign Policy

Vivasvan Shastri
Yesha Bhatt
Series Editor
Arun Anand

PRABHAT
PAPERBACKS

Published by
PRABHAT PAPERBACKS
4/19 Asaf Ali Road,
New Delhi-110 002 (INDIA)
e-mail: prabhatbooks@gmail.com

ISBN 978-93-5266-985-1
DYNAMIC DIPLOMACY & FOREIGN POLICY
by Vivasvan Shastri and Yesha Bhatt

Edition
First, 2018

Price
₹ 150.00 (Rupees One Hundred Fifty only)

Printed at
R-Tech Offset Printers, Delhi

'Welfare of state depends on an active Foreign Policy.'

—Chanakya

Editorial Note

Transforming India

The idea of 'Transforming India' series germinated a few months ago when we were approaching the fourth anniversary of Narendra Modi led National Democratic Alliance government at the Centre. The responsibility to conceptualise and execute this plan was entrusted to me as Editor of this series. I have been ably assisted by a team of writers and researchers to execute this project.

Initially we planned a series of three books covering the first four years of Modi government at the Centre.

One of the key reasons for doing this series was to objectively assess the performance of this government on various fronts as there seems to be a concerted effort to take the national debate away from issues related to the governance.

For a thriving democracy which has the largest pool of youth in the world, what matters at the end of the day is whether a government has done enough to transform the country which is at the cusp of becoming a super power in the global power structure.

India, today, is an aspirational nation. The expectations from Modi government have been very high. We have tried to do a reality check through this series of books i.e. how Modi government has fared in terms of meeting the expectations of the people of India.

With bold moves like demonetisation and implementation of the Goods and Services Tax, Modi government has taken a huge political risk by attempting to break the status-quo. There are few governments in the history of independent India who have pro-actively used the diplomacy to pursue India's geo-political and economic interests globally by engaging with the leading nations in the world power matrix at equal footing.

The tenure of Modi led government would go down into the history of our country as one of the most interesting chapters which had long lasting impact on the national life and India's global positioning. Thus it was important to document what all this government had done on the issue of governance.

The writers of this series have done commendable work as it wasn't an easy task to take out key events and policies from a huge pool of initiatives taken by this government. We hope that this series would be a ready reckoner for those who want to know what Modi government did in some of the key sectors. This is not an all exhaustive series as we have taken select areas and hence many more areas are left to be covered.

We hope the readers would also be able to use this series as reference material. We look forward to your valuable feedback.

New Delhi
July, 2018

—Arun Anand

Foreword

"One vision I can see clear as life before me is that the ancient Mother has awakened once more, sitting on her throne-rejuvenated, more glorious than ever. Proclaim her to the entire world with the voice of peace and benediction." – Swami Vivekananda.

Swami Vivekananda wanted a resurrected India that would be the leader of the world (*vishwa guru* Bharat).

India as a nation has engaged the world effectively for thousands of years on two fronts – economic and cultural. Early engagement of India with the world was economic in nature. Trade and shipping routes linked India to the rest of the world. Trade in spices and silk made India a sought after destination. Import and export of goods linked India and the world.

Economic engagement with the world was followed by cultural engagement. Arts, music and way of life found acceptance in all parts of the world. Buddhism found acceptance in China, Japan and many other parts of the world.

India was also the most favoured destination for learning. It was very common to see the best and brightest of the world make their way to Nalanda and Takshashila. India was also the destination for royals in Asia to send their future kings and queens for learning and grooming.

Over the last 1,000 years, India had been occupied and

colonised. The economic and cultural bonds that Indian civilisation had established with the rest of world were usurped by the occupying forces for their own needs. India's economic and cultural bonds with the world weakened and were made virtually non-existent.

Despite the economic and cultural isolation, India's contribution to the world in the last century has been significant. Indian soldiers fought both the World Wars in large numbers. India makes a significant contribution to the United Nations peace-keeping force. Indian diaspora all across the world makes a positive contribution to the society and the country they live in.

India's foreign policy over the last 71 years of independence can be categorised in three phases. Jawaharlal Nehru set the tone in the first phase for non-alignment and economic independence which were the key principles of our foreign policy.

India refused to engage with the global powers (the US and the Soviet Union) and was more keen in building a third non-aligned alliance. This third alliance had neither the economic clout nor any say in global affairs. India lost an opportunity to find a permanent seat in the United Nations Security Council when Nehru offered the seat to China. India fought many wars but was left to defend herself alone. There was little global support when India had to face China and Pakistan.

Indian economy remained isolated from the rest of the world. While the global economy prospered, India struggled against poverty. Cultural engagement with the world was put on a back burner.

Under Indira Gandhi, India's foreign policy acquired a pro-Soviet shift. This policy virtually forced the US and

China to align with Pakistan. Both economic and cultural engagement with the world remained weak.

The second phase of our foreign policy dawned as the Soviet Union collapsed. The Gulf War of 1990 left India on the verge of bankruptcy. In the second phase, India was forced to engage the world on economic terms to ensure her own survival. Coalition governments were a norm and as the Central Government became weak and as state leaders called the shots, foreign policy took a backseat.

With the election of Atal Bihari Vajpayee, foreign policy returned to centre stage. Vajpayee boldly conducted nuclear tests and effectively countered the economic sanctions imposed on India.

Vajpayee defined the roadmap for India-US relations when both became natural allies. He improved relations with China and set a new paradigm for engaging with Pakistan. Vajpayee was the first Prime Minister to break away from the non-aligned mindset.

With reforms under Vajpayee government and no hangover of being non-aligned, India confidently engaged with the world. India's economy was now fully linked with the global economy and we saw years of high growth.

Manmohan Singh inherited a foreign policy which was robust and strong. However as he lacked the mandate from his own party as well as from allies, there was little to no progress on the foreign policy front. Voices of non-alignment re-surfaced again. Despite the US administration offering India a civil nuclear deal on a platter, India was unable to clinch it. China was getting increasingly assertive and Pakistan got so bold as to launch an assault on Mumbai. It felt that our foreign policy was toothless and inactive.

The 2014 national election was fought on domestic

issues. Narendra Modi started the campaign with a double handicap on foreign policy. He had little foreign policy experience. He had also been denied a visa by the USA and many countries in Europe had kept an arms distance from him. Given that the foreign policy under the UPA was in tatters, not much was expected from the Modi government.

With the election of Prime Minister Narendra Modi in 2014 with an absolute majority, the stage was set for the third phase of our foreign policy. He won in 2014 on the plank of development and growth. To promote growth, he chose to re-energise economic engagement with the world.

Modi also took the bold step of re-introducing cultural engagement as an important principle of foreign policy. Indian diaspora are now seen as cultural ambassadors of a great civilisation.

India's foreign policy in this phase has been bold and confident. This third phase of our foreign policy uses economic and cultural engagement as key principles in engaging with the world.

This book analyses the performance of Modi in re-rejuvenating India's foreign policy. We also benchmark Prime Minister Narendra Modi's performance with Swami Vivekananda's vision of making India a *'vishwa guru'*.

Yesha Bhatt
Twitter: @BhattYesha_

Vivasvan Shastri
e-mail: vivasvan@me.com
Twitter: @VivaShastri
Facebook: https://www.facebook.com/viva.shastri
blog: http://vivabunchofthoughts.blogspot.in.

Contents

1
Neighbourhood First

Former Prime Minister, Atal Bihari Vajpayee had once remarked, "You can change your friends but not your neighbours".

India shares a lot more with her neighbours than just borders. We have a shared history and a common language or culture. India and her neighbours are collectively referred to as a subcontinent. However, there has been far less integration, be it economic or cultural between India and her neighbours in the last many decades

India has land, river and maritime disputes with many of her neighbours. In many countries, India is not seen as a friend but at times as a bully, with a big brother attitude. Even after 71 years of independence, India's foreign policy has not been able to unite the subcontinent into an integrated cohesive unit that can collectively engage with the global powers.

During the last ten years of the UPA government, India's relationship with her neighbours continued to decline. Manmohan Singh had inherited a robust foreign policy from Atal Bihari Vajpayee. The NDA government had re-defined the paradigm of Indo-Pak relations by agreeing to discuss Kashmir, encourage people-to-people contact and further economic integration.

India and China under Atal Bihari Vajpayee had agreed on a framework to resolve all boundary issues.

The UPA government squandered all these advantages in no time. Manmohan Singh was not allowed by his ally, the DMK to engage with Sri Lanka. In 2013, when the Commonwealth Heads of Government Meeting (CHOGM) was held in Colombo, Manmohan Singh was not allowed to attend the meeting due to pressure from the DMK. India was forced to vote against Sri Lanka at the United Nations. This refusal to engage with Sri Lanka virtually forced Sri Lanka into the arms of China.

India's Bangladesh policy was held hostage by the West Bengal state government and its mercurial leader Mamata Banerjee. Even though Bangladesh was more than eager to resolve all issues on land or water sharing, Manmohan Singh could never get Mamata Banerjee on board.

With Pakistan, Manmohan Singh did continue with the back channel dialogue that was started by Atal Bihari Vajpayee. But a weak government was very scared of cutting a deal with Pakistan for it was very worried that it may not be able to get the domestic audience on board on any deal.

In dealing with China, the UPA government did not realise that since the agreement of a framework with Atal Bihari Vajpayee, China had modernised its army and also built its infrastructure in the border regions with India. A strong China wanted to re-negotiate with India. The UPA government was at a complete loss on how to deal with China.

Thus a confused UPA government held hostage by its allies was only able to create distance and distrust between India and her neighbours. A subcontinent with a shared history and culture was now reduced to a group of countries with numerous disputes. India's neighbourhood policy was in shambles. This can be gauged by the number of trips Manmohan Singh made to the neighbourhood countries during his 10-year tenure. The trips were too few and far between. To make it worse, nothing substantive was achieved.

China had by now built strong relationships with India's neighbours. China's massive investments in India's neighbourhood along with India's inability to effectively engage with them had many security analysts worried. Many called it China's geo-political encirclement of India.

Narendra Modi was the first Prime Minister to be elected with a complete majority in 30 years. He was keenly aware that foreign policy begins with neighbours. His first masterstroke on foreign policy played out even before he took the oath – he invited all of India's neighbours, including Mauritius, to his swearing-in ceremony on 26th May 2014.

The invitation sent out a clear message — the first principle of Modi's foreign policy was neighbourhood first. Key tenets of integrating the subcontinent were clearly spelt, out i.e. economic and cultural.

There were murmurs and protests within India on Narendra Modi's invitation to the heads of Pakistan and Sri Lanka. He even before taking oath made one thing clear – our nation's foreign policy will be driven by the Prime Minister and not outsourced to allies. India's national interest will take precedence over state-level electoral issues.

By inviting Mauritius, Modi highlighted India's special relationship with the island nation and the people of Indian origin living there. He had also realised the geo-political significance of Mauritius in safeguarding the Indian Ocean.

The move also highlighted Modi's understanding of

geo-politics. A united, integrated and powerful subcontinent would only strengthen him to engage the United States and China. A strong and secure subcontinent is critical to a strong and secure India. A strong Prime Minister also had the mandate to make tough decisions that were required to begin the process of integrating the subcontinent.

It was for the first time in history that the swearing-in ceremony of the Prime Minister of India had all the SAARC countries in attendance. Afghanistan was represented by President Hamid Karzai. Speaker of Bangladesh Shirin Sharmin Chaudhary attended on behalf of Prime Minister Sheikh Hasina as she had a pre-planned visit to Japan. Prime Minister Tshering Tobgay attended the ceremony and also had bilateral discussions with Prime Minister Modi on 27th May 2014.

Maldives President Abdulla Yameen Abdul Gayoom. Mauritius Prime Minister Navin Ramgoolam, Nepal Prime Minister Sushil Koirala were also in attendance.

Pakistan Prime Minister Nawaz Sharif made it to the event despite domestic compulsions and pressures.

Source: mea.gov.in

Political parties from Tamil Nadu had spoken against Modi's decision to invite the Sri Lankan president. MDMK chief Vaiko met Modi to try to change his mind and Congress too joined hands with him.

Prime Minister Narendra Modi's first test on foreign policy presented itself even before he had taken the oath. But he proved his mettle by going ahead with his invitation. This act of statesmanship from a newly appointed Prime Minister showed results with both Pakistan and Sri Lanka announcing the release of Indian fishermen held in captivity.

Also in attendance was Prime Minister of Tibetan government-in-exile, Lobsang Sangay, even though the Chinese government opposed the invitation to the Tibetan leader.

With his swearing-in ceremony, Prime Minister Modi sent a clear message to the global community — a strong leader with a strong mandate had taken oath. India's foreign policy and her engagement with the world would now change gears.

Prime Minister Narendra Modi's move to invite all the SAARC leaders was hailed in capitals around the world. The swearing-in ceremony set the tone on foreign policy.

Prime Minister Modi's swearing-in ceremony made it to the editorials globally.

'Narendra Modi sworn in as Indian Prime Minister, Heralding Change," said the headline of the *Los Angeles Times*.

The *Wall Street Journal said*: "Narendra Modi, the son of a tea-seller with political roots in India's Hindu nationalist movement, was sworn in as Prime Minister of the world's largest democracy, putting in place a leaner Central Government and promising Indians 'a glorious future'.

"Getting India's economy growing at a faster clip will be a top priority for Mr. Modi, who was propelled to power by voters who want better job opportunities, higher standards of living and a more efficient government," it said.

The Journal added that some analysts say that Modi is likely to make major decisions from the Prime Minister's office. "That would mark a departure from former Prime Minister Manmohan Singh's more hands-off governing style," it said.

The *Chicago Tribune* said for the first time, India invited the heads of state of the entire eight-nation SAARC to the ceremony and all sent representatives.

Let us now look at how Prime Minister Narendra Modi transformed India's relationships with her neighbouring countries.

Transforming Ties with Bangladesh

'The last few years were a golden period in India-Bangladesh ties'.

—Narendra Modi

India and Bangladesh share history, culture and even a language. India is also the largest neighbour of Bangladesh with a shared border of approximately 4,000 km. It was at the strategic intervention of India that Bangladesh achieved independence from Pakistan

Bangladesh is moreover critical for India to establish a seamless link with the South-east Asian countries. India and Bangladesh are also members of members of SAARC, BIMSTEC, IORA and the Commonwealth.

The first destination of the External Affairs Minister, Sushma Swaraj was Dhaka. Bangladesh had begun to see India as an unreliable partner. Sheikh Hasina had gone out of the way to address the security concerns highlighted by New Delhi. India did reciprocate by removing tariffs on goods imported by India from Bangladesh.

In September 2011, when Manmohan Singh visited Dhaka, there was hope and optimism. Dhaka and New

Delhi had agreed on a framework to resolve the Teesta as well as the boundary issue. The Chief Minister of West Bengal Mamata Banerjee opposed the signing of the Teesta agreement and diplomatic relationship between India and Bangladesh received a severe setback.

Manmohan Singh did sign the Land Boundary Agreement but could not get it ratified in Parliament. It became hard for Bangladesh to trust any commitment by India. Both India and Bangladesh had hoped to transform their relationship but it ended in disappointment for both sides.

The first opportunity for the Modi government to set things right with Bangladesh presented itself in July 2014. India and Bangladesh had a long time maritime territorial dispute and the international tribunal at The Hague was expected to give a verdict.

India had two choices — one was to behave like China and reject any decision of the international tribunal; the second choice; was to accept the verdict as a win-win scenario for both India and Bangladesh and leverage it to deepen integration.

The statesman in Prime Minister Narendra Modi quickly decided to accept the verdict. Dhaka too responded in kind. India's response to the verdict was that of an emerging global power which was sensitive to the needs of her neighbours for the greater good of the region.

Partition of India had left many enclaves within India and Bangladesh. People living in enclaves were so trapped they could not access any services from their respective governments.

According to a joint census conducted by both the countries, there are 111 Bangladeshi enclaves in India that house 37,369 people, while 14,215 people have been residing in 55 Indian enclaves in Bangladesh. Any agreement between India and Bangladesh would impact the states of Assam, Tripura, West Bengal and Meghalaya. The agreement with Bangladesh will mean the exchange of a series of enclaves. Assam alone will have to hand over 250 acres.

Manmohan Singh had signed the border dispute agreement with Bangladesh but could not get the Indian Parliament to ratify it. Manmohan Singh had in fact requested Mamata Banerjee to accompany him during his 2011 visit to Bangladesh; Mamata had then declined.

Prime Minister Narendra Modi not only got all the states on boardbut also got the Indian Parliament to ratify it. In June 2017, he made history by operationalising the boundary agreement with Bangladesh. Not only was a 40-year-old issue resolved, but trust was re-established between New Delhi and Dhaka..

Speaking at a joint briefing with his Bangladeshi counterpart, the Prime Minister said, "The visit is at a historic moment. We have resolved a question that has lingered since Independence. Our two nations have a settled boundary. It will make our borders more secure and people's life there more stable. Our Parliament's approval of Land Boundary Agreement reflects the consensus in India on relations with Bangladesh."

"We accepted the settlement of the maritime boundary last year. It is evidence of the maturity of our ties and our shared commitment to international rules. So, we stand at a moment of huge opportunity in our relationship. Prime Minister (Sheikh Hasina) and I recognise that."

"We will work together to harness the rich potential of our relationship. And, we will address our challenges in a spirit of friendship and from a position of mutual trust and confidence," Modi said.

Modi also emphasised the importance of trade and commerce between the two countries.

In his statement, he said, "Now, we are successful fellow-travellers on the road to development. Our growing co-operation is a picture of my deeply held belief in the shared prosperity of neighbours. That is why the future I dream for India is the future I wish for Bangladesh."

"As we deepen our political engagement and celebrate our rich inheritance, as our economies get more integrated and our people better connected, our nations will become more prosperous. It will also open new economic doors for India's northeast. And, it will enable our two countries to integrate South Asia and connect it with the dynamic east," he added.

The Prime Minister also announced a new line of credit of $2 billion to Bangladesh.

Announcing this, he said, "Our development partnership is scaling new heights. The quick implementation of the line of credit of $800 million and full disbursement of $200 million in grant is a tribute to our co-operation. We are pleased to extend another line of credit of $2 billion to support infrastructure and other development activities in Bangladesh."

Modi also expressed his optimism about the two countries' co-operation to prevent illegal activities.

He said, "As the three agreements on human trafficking, fake Indian currency and maritime safety show, our security co-operation is growing. I am confident that we both have the political will and mutual confidence to further improve border management and coordination to prevent illegal activities, trafficking and movements."

Accompanying Prime Minister Narendra Modi on his trip was the Chief Minister of Bengal, Mamata Banerjee. The statesmanship of a true leader was on full display.

India and Bangladesh are now working on improving connectivity – via roads, railways, international waterways or coastal shipping. India and Bangladesh are working in tandem to address many of issues facing the subcontinent. One such example is the Rohingya refugee crisis where both India and Bangladesh are working with Myanmar to resolve the issues.

Ties between Bangladesh and India have now been transformed for the good. Our neighbour is now our well-wisher and friend.

Nepal

Prime Minister Modi, during his visit to Nepal in 2018, summarised the eternal bonds between India and Nepal beautifully:

"नेपाल के बिना हमारे धाम अधूरे और राम भी"

In English it translates to "Without Nepal, neither are our holy places or Lord Rama complete". This eloquent quote beautifully summarises the family, cultural, spiritual and cultural bonds that have bonded India and Nepal for thousands of years.

Nepal finds a mention in the *itihaas* of Bharat - the *Ramayana*. Sita was born and brought up in Nepal. King Janak from Nepal is idealised as a learned and wise king. There are spiritual linkages that go back in history too. Pashupatinath is likened to Kashi Vishwanath, Lumbini with Bodh Gaya, Janakpur with Ayodhya and Guhyeshwari with Kamkhya.

India and Nepal also have a shared sacred geography –

the Himalayas. Indian Army has some of its roots in Nepal. The Gurkha regiment finds its recruits from Nepal. Even today we find many retired Indian army personnel settled in Nepal but earning their pensions from India.

Lastly, the economic bonds between India and Nepal are very strong. Trade done by Nepal mostly goes via India. Close to 8 million Nepali citizens are employed in India. A Nepali citizen is free to work, live and buy property in India.

It is therefore very surprising that there is a perception in Nepal that India does not respect Nepal's sovereignty and tends to interfere in the domestic issues of Nepal.

During the UPA tenure, the Manmohan Singh government misread the mood of the people of Nepal and supported an unpopular monarchy. It was comical that on the same day that Prime Minister Manmohan Singh was advocating a role for monarchy along with parliamentary democracy in Nepal, his own diplomat Shyam Saran held a press conference where he indicated that India would not interfere in domestic issues of Nepal and was comfortable with the idea of getting rid of the monarchy.

India's stance of standing with monarchy was surprising as the monarchy in Nepal had for generations warmed up to China while projecting India as a bully. During the UPA tenure, India's spiritual and cultural ally was often taken for granted.

In the last four years, Prime Minister Modi has managed to build trust and re-kindle the eternal alliance.

Prime Ministers Nepal's policy can be summed up using 3Ds:

Dharma – Re-kindle the spiritual bonds. Prime Minister's visits to the Pashupatinath temple, Janaki Mandir, etc. send a very powerful message to the people of Nepal, i.e.

we share common values and a way of life. Trust can only be built on shared values and there are no two countries which have more in common than India and Nepal. This is also a powerful antidote to China whose only relationship with Nepal is based on economic incentives.

Development – India not only provides employment to 8 million Nepalis but is also its critical trading partner. India's energy needs can be met by Nepal's focus on hydroelectricity. Nepal, like Bhutan, can also prosper by being an energy partner to India. Recently, key agreements were signed with a focus to improve connectivity via road, rail and waterways. In addition, India would support Nepal in modernising agriculture.

Democracy – India today stands as a true partner as Nepal begins its journey as a republic which is governed by a constitution that supports a multi-party democracy.

India played a critical role in providing relief to Nepal post the 2015 earthquake. According to a press release by the Ministry of External Affairs:

"When a devastating 7.8 magnitude earthquake struck Nepal on 25 April 2015 (followed by a powerful aftershock of 7.4 magnitude on 12 May 2015), the Government of India swiftly dispatched National Disaster Response Force (NDRF) teams and special aircraft with rescue and relief material to Nepal. India's assistance, which reached Nepal within six hours of the earthquake, included 16 NDRF teams, 39 IAF aircraft sorties with 571 tons of relief material including rescue equipment, medical supplies, food, water, tents, blankets and tarpaulin. Medical teams from India were deployed in various parts of Nepal. India helped in restoring three power sub–stations in Kathmandu valley. The total Indian relief assistance to Nepal amounted to approximately US$ 67 million. The Government of India had announced a post–earthquake reconstruction package of US$ 1 bn (which comprises US$ 250 million grant and US$ 750 millionconcessional line of credit) during the International Conference on Nepal's Reconstruction held in Kathmandu on 25 June 2015. During the visit of Prime Minister of Nepal, Mr Pushpa Kamal Dahal 'Prachanda' to India from 15-18 September 2016, a mandatory agreement to US$ 1bn line of credit agreement signed on 25 November 2014, enabling reapportioning of unutilised funds for post-earthquake reconstruction projects in Nepal and a New Line of Credit agreement for US$ 750 million for post-earthquake reconstruction projects in Nepal were signed."

Indian firms are the biggest investors in Nepal, accounting for about 40 per cent of the total approved foreign direct investments. There are about 150 Indian ventures operating in Nepal. They are engaged in manufacturing, services (banking, insurance, dry port, education and telecom), power sector and tourism industries.

Modi has managed to win the hearts of the people of Nepal. This can be gauged by his personal popularity in Nepal and the reception he gets from the locals during his visits.

Foreign policy experts have also noted the progress made by the Modi government in not only restoring ties with Nepal but also effectively countering China's moves.

"Countering hard power by projecting soft power — In contrast to China's efforts to muscle its way into Nepal, Modi's current, well-received visit to the Himalayan nation seeks to emphasise India's historically close cultural, religious and people-to-people relations with Nepal," said Brahma Chellaney, analyst with the New Delhi-based Centre for Policy Research think-tank in a Twitter post.

Sri Lanka

Like Nepal and Bangladesh, Sri Lanka also shares spiritual, cultural and linguistic links to India. Nearly 70 per cent of the people of Sri Lanka follows Buddhism. It was in the 4th century BCE that the son of Emperor Ashoka, Mahinda introduced Buddhism to Sri Lanka. A sapling from the Bodhi tree was brought to Sri Lanka and monasteries were established. The Tamil-minority population of Sri Lanka has cultural and linguistic ties with the people of Tamil Nadu.

Sri Lanka also finds a mention in our *itihaas* the *Ramayana*. India is also Sri Lanka's only neighbour connected by the Ramsethu. It is believed that the relationship between India and Sri Lanka is more than 2,500 years old. Both Sri Lanka and India are strategically placed in the Indian Ocean through which much of the world trade is conducted.

It was India's participation in the Sri Lankan civil war that soured the relationship with Sri Lanka. Even post the civil war, the UPA government under Manmohan Singh refused to effectively engage with Sri Lanka due to pressure from allies. Manmohan Singh was even denied permission to visit Sri Lanka for a Commonwealth Summit. In the recent past, Sri Lanka has moved closer to China which has promised the development of ports. In lieu, Chinese submarines have been allowed to dock in Sri Lankan ports.

Modi's swearing-in ceremony was a bold start. Prime Minister Modi stood by his invitation to the Sri Lankan President despite opposition from regional political parties. Post his election, the relationship between India and Sri Lanka have constantly improved.

President Maithripala Sirisena was elected as the new President of Sri Lanka in the presidential election held on 8 January 2015. Following the parliamentary elections on 17

August 2015, Ranil Wickremesinghe was reappointed as the Prime Minister by President Sirisena on 21 August 2015.

While the UPA government refused to effectively engage with Sri Lanka, in the last three years, we have seen regular meetings with the Heads of State. According to a report by Ministry of External Affairs:

President Sirisena paid a four-day visit to India starting 15 February 2015. President Sirisena visited India on 13-14 May 2016 on a working visit. During the visit, he visited New Delhi, Ujjain and Sanchi. He travelled to India on 19-21 August 2016 on a private visit. President Sirisena travelled to India on 15-17 October 2016 to attend the BRICS-BIMSTEC Outreach Summit. President Sirisena travelled to India on 6-7 November 2016 to attend the seventh session of the Conference of Parties (COP7) to World Health Organisation (WHO) Framework Convention on Tobacco Control (FCTC) in New Delhi. Prime Minister Ranil Wickremesinghe visited India in September 2015, his first overseas visit after being appointed Prime Minister.

"President Sirisena and Prime Minister Shri Narendra Modi also met on the margins of the 70th session of UNGA in New York in September 2015 and at the COP21 meeting at Paris in November 2015. Prime Minister Wickremesinghe travelled to India on 4-6th October 2016 for the India Economic Summit. He again paid a working visit to India from 25-29th April 2017 and an MOU on co-operation in economic projects was signed during the visit. Regular ministerial visits from Sri Lanka to India are taking place. Few are listed as follows; Foreign Minister Mangala Samaraweera visited New Delhi in January 2015 on his first overseas official visit. Speaker Karu Jayasuriya visited India to participate in the 5th International Buddhist Conclave in New Delhi on 2 October

2016. He also attended the South Asian Speakers Summit on Achieving the Sustainable Development Goals organised by the Parliament of India and Inter-Parliamentary Union in Indore on 18-20 February 2017. Former Foreign Minister Ravi Karunanayake visited India on his first overseas visit on 6-7 June 2017. Newly appointed Foreign Minister Tilak Marapana visited India from 8-10 September 2017. This was his first overseas official visit after assuming charge.

"Prime Minister Narendra Modi visited Sri Lanka on 13-14 March, 2015. He travelled to Anuradhapura, Talaimannar, and Jaffna. He again visited Sri Lanka on 11-12 May 2017 as a chief guest to attend the International Day of Vesak celebrations in Sri Lanka. During the visit, he inaugurated Dickoya Hospital, addressed a gathering in Norwood's ground and took blessings at Sri Dalada Maligawa temple in Kandy. Sumitra Mahajan, Speaker of Lok Sabha visited Sri Lanka from 02-07 October 2017 to attend a special parliamentary session in celebration of 70th anniversary of the establishment of Parliament of Sri Lanka on 3 October 2017 and to attend the 8th Conference of the Association of SAARC Speakers and Parliamentarians held in Colombo from 4-6 October 2017.

External Affairs Minister Sushma Swaraj led an inter-ministerial delegation to Colombo from 5-6 February 2016 for the 9th session of the India-Sri Lanka Joint Commission. Earlier, she was in Colombo on 6-7 March 2015 to prepare for Prime Minister's visit. She led a 12-member parliamentary delegation to Sri Lanka in April 2012 as the then leader of Opposition in the Lok Sabha. EAM visited 31 August 1 September 2017 to attend the second Indian Ocean Conference organised in Colombo. Commerce and Industry Minister Nirmala Sitharaman visited Sri Lanka on 26-27

September 2016. Minister of State for External Affairs Gen. V.K. Singh (Retd) visited Colombo from 24-26 August 2016 to participate in the Fifth Ministerial Meeting of the Colombo Process. Foreign Secretary Dr S. Jaishankar visited Sri Lanka from 12-13 January 2016, for bilateral discussions with Sri Lankan leaders. He, accompanied by a business delegation visited Sri Lanka from 22-24 October 2016. Foreign Secretary again visited Sri Lanka from 18-20 February 2017, 4-6 April 2017 and 31 August 1 September 2017.

On 18 June 2016 Prime Minister and President Maithripala Sirisena, through video conferencing from New Delhi, jointly inaugurated the newly renovated Duraiappah Stadium in Jaffna. A mega yoga event at this stadium launched the week-long yoga celebrations for 2016 in Sri Lanka. The event was a performance of 'Surya Namaskar' by almost 11,000 school children. On 28 July, Prime Minister delivered a video message at a ceremony to launch Emergency Ambulance Service in Colombo, set up with Indian financial assistance. Prime Minister Wickremesinghe launched the services in Colombo"

As seen from the MEA report, regular and meaningful dialogue have been established between India and Sri Lanka at all levels. Gone are the days when the Prime Minister of India had to take permission from a local ally to travel to Sri Lanka.

According to MEA, India is among the top four investors in Sri Lanka with cumulative investments of over US$ 1 billion since 2003. The investments are in diverse areas including petroleum retail, IT, financial services, real estate, telecommunication, hospitality and tourism, banking and food processing (tea and fruit juices), metal industries, tires, cement, glass manufacturing and infrastructure development (railway, power, water supply).

A number of new investments from Indian companies are in the pipeline or under implementation. Notable among them are proposals of South City, Kolkata for real estate development in Colombo (US $ 400 million), Tata Housing Slave Island Development project along with Urban Development Authority of Sri Lanka (US $ 430 million), and 'Colombo One' project of ITC Ltd. (ITC has committed an investment of US$ 300 million, augmenting the earlier committed US 140 million). Dabur set up a fruit-juice-manufacturing plant (US$ 17 million) in May 2013.

On the other hand, the last few years have also witnessed an increasing trend of Sri Lankan investments in India. Significant examples include Brandix (about US$ 1 billion to set up a garment city in Visakhapatnam), MAS holdings, John Keels, Hayleys, and Aitken Spence (Hotels), apart from other investments in the freight servicing and logistics sector.

Sri Lanka is one of the major recipients of development credit from the Government of India, with atotal commitment of around US$ 2.63 billion, including US$ 458 million as grants. Under a line of credit of $ 167.4 million, the tsunami-damaged Colombo-Matara rail link has been repaired and upgraded. Another line of credit of $ 800 million for track laying and supply of rolling stock to support construction railway lines in northern Sri Lanka is already operational.

India also continues to assist a large number of smaller development projects in spheres like education, health, transport connectivity, small and medium enterprise development and training in many parts of the country through its grant funding.

On 21 June 2015, the First International Day of Yoga was celebrated at the iconic oceanside promenade, Galle Face Green. The event was attended by two thousand yoga enthusiasts. In 2016, a similar event was organised at Mahavihara Devi Park to celebrate International Day of Yoga. Celebrations of the 3rd International Day of Yoga have already started in Sri Lanka by way of curtain-raiser event as also various road shows in different cities of Sri Lanka. Every year, cultural troupes from both countries exchange visits. Pursuant to an announcement made by the Prime Minister during his visit to Sri Lanka, a Festival of India in Sri Lanka was launched in November 2015, with 'Nrityarupa', a scintillating dance medley from different parts of India, performed in Colombo, Kandy and Galle. The theme of the Festival was Sangam: a confluence of cultures of India and Sri Lanka.

In the last four years, Modi's foreign policy has strengthened India's relationship with Sri Lanka. Lack of engagement and trust have been replaced by strong economic and cultural bonds which will strengthen the 2,500-year-old relationship.

Bhutan

India and Bhutan have enjoyed strong diplomatic relations since 1968. The first country to be visited by Prime Minister Narendra Modi was Bhutan in June 2014. According to the Ministry of External Affairs:

"The visit reinforced the tradition of regular high-level exchanges between the two countries. He addressed the joint session of Bhutanese Parliament on 16 June2014. During the visit, he laid the foundation stone of the 600 MW Kholongchhu Hydropower Project and inaugurated the Supreme Court building which was constructed with Government of India's assistance. Besides exchanging views and discussing bilateral relations and economic co-operation, Prime Minister Modi announced doubling of the Nehru Wangchuck Scholarship to ₹ 2 crores per year. He also announced Government of India's assistance for the establishment of an E-library covering all the 20 districts of Bhutan."

Hydropower projects in Bhutan are an example of win-win co-operation, providing a reliable source of inexpensive and clean electricity to India, generating export revenue for Bhutan and cementing our economic integration. So far, the Government of India has constructed three hydroelectric projects in Bhutan totalling 1416 MW (336 MW Chukha HEP, 60 MW Kurichhu HEP and 1020 MW Tala HEP), which are operational and exporting surplus power to India. About three-fourths of the power generated is exported and rest is used for domestic consumption. Hydropower exports provide more than 40 per cent of Bhutan's domestic revenue and constitute 25 per cent of its GDP.

In June 2017, China attempted to extend a road southward in Doklam which is in Bhutan. Around 270 Indian troops entered Doklam to make an attempt to stop the construction the road. India had never made claims over Doklam but in support of her ally, Bhutan, rushed its troops. Chinese media threatened war and even reminded India of the 1962 defeat. India stood ground and eventually resolved the issue, with China withdrawing its troops from Doklam in August 2017.

The Doklam standoff and eventual diplomatic resolution signalled to the entire region that they can count on India as an ally. It raised the stature of the Prime Minister as a true global leader to have the nerve and courage to stand up for an ally and take on China.

Myanmar

Myanmar and India share a border of over 1600 km. Indian states of Arunachal Pradesh, Nagaland, Manipur and Mizoram share a boundary with Myanmar. India also shares a maritime boundary with Myanmar. Both India and Myanmar also have a shared heritage of religious, linguistic and ethnic ties. Myanmar is also the only ASEAN country adjoining India and is hence the gateway to South-east Asia and is critical to India's 'Act East' policy of engaging with the ASEAN countries.

Myanmar President U Htin Kyaw undertook a state visit to India from 27-30 August2016. During the visit, President U Htin Kyaw held wide-ranging discussions with Prime Minister Modi. Four documents were signed: MOU on co-operation in traditional medicine, renewable energy, construction of 69 bridges in the Tamu-Kyigone-Kalewa section and co-operation in the construction of Kalewa-Yagyi road section of the same trilateral highway.

State Counsellor, Daw Aung San Suu Kyi undertook a state visit to India on 17- 19 at October 2016 after participating in the BRICS-BIMSTEC Outreach Summit on 16 October at Goa, when she met the President of India, Prime Minister and External Affairs Minister. Three MOUs on power, insurance and banking supervision were signed. India assured support for the creation of livelihoods, upgradeskills, reconstruction of roads, power, education facilities and health infrastructure for the Myanmar people.

Defence and security co-operation has strengthened over the years. Exchange of high-level visits, the signing of MoU on border co-operation, talks on the training of Army, Air Force and Naval staff talks are important indicators in this direction.

According to the Ministry of External Affairs:

"India and Myanmar share close cultural ties and a sense of deep kinship given India's Buddhist heritage.

Building on this shared heritage, India is undertaking some key initiatives, like restoration of the Ananda Temple in Bagan and donation of a 16-foot replica of the Sarnath Buddha statue which has been installed at the premises of Shwedagon pagoda in Yangon.

The 'Samvad-II' interfaith Dialogue was held on 6-7th August 2017 at Yangon. The event was graced by Shri Ram Naik, Governor of Uttar Pradesh, Shri Yogi Adityanath, Chief Minister of Uttar Pradesh and MoS, Home Affairs, Shri Kiren Rejiju. ICCR and Sitagu International Buddhist Academy organised an international conference on Buddhist Cultural Heritage from 15-17 December 2012. Performances by cultural troupes were organised on a regular basis. Myanmar troupes and artists have participated in South Asian and ASEAN cultural events in India.

India has responded to Myanmar's interest in restoring and renovating two historic temples in Bodh Gaya built by Myanmar rulers, King Mindon and King Baygyidaw. These temples and inscriptions will now be restored with the assistance of the Archaeological Survey of India as a bilateral friendship project."

In January 2018, India signed an agreement between India and Myanmar on land border crossing which the government said would enhance economic interaction between the people of the two countries.

Maldives

Maldives is strategically located in the Indian Ocean and ties with Male are of special importance to India. Recent political events in Maldives have strained relations with India but the Modi government has done a good job is staying away from local domestic events. India's policy remains to engage with her neighbours on economic and cultural terms while not interfering in domestic issues.

Modi's government has done an outstanding job in providing humanitarian aid. In the wake of a drinking water crisis in Male on 4 December 2014, following the collapse of the island's only water-treatment plant, Maldives urged India for immediate help. India came to its rescue by sending its heavy lift transporters like C-17 Globemaster III, Il-76 carrying bottled water. The Navy also sent her ships, like *'INS Sukanya', 'INS Deepak'* and others which can produce fresh water using their onboard desalination plants. The humanitarian relief effort by the Indian side was widely appreciated in Male across all sections of the people; even the Vice-President of Maldives thanked the Indian ambassador for swift action.

Afghanistan

India and Afghanistan have a strong relationship based on historical and cultural links. The relationship is not limited to the governments in New Delhi and Kabul but has its foundations in the historical contacts and exchanges between the people.

According to the Ministry of External Affairs:

"On 4 June 2016, Prime Minister visited Herat in western Afghanistan and he, along with President Ghani, jointly inaugurated the Afghan-India Friendship Dam, earlier known as Salma Dam. The completion of the dam project represents the culmination of years of hard work by about 1,500 Indian and Afghan engineers and other professionals in very difficult conditions. It also highlights India's continued commitment to Afghanistan's reconstruction and development.

"On 22 August 2016, Prime Minister Narendra Modi

jointly inaugurated through video conferencing the restored Stor Palace in Kabul with President Ghani. During his speech, the Indian Prime Minister said that the 1.25 billion Indian people will 'always' stand with Afghanistan in ensuring peace and prosperity.

"On 25 December 2016, Prime Minister Narendra Modi along with a high-level delegation paid a visit to Afghanistan. During his visit he called on President Ashraf Ghani; he met Chief Executive, Dr Abdullah and former President Hamid Karzai. During his visit, he inaugurated the newly built Afghan Parliament; announced 500 scholarships for children of the martyrs of Afghan Security Forces and gifted four Mi-25 attack helicopters to the Afghan Air Force. During the visit, it was also decided to conduct the second Strategic Partnership Council meeting headed by the Foreign Ministers of both countries in the first quarter of 2016 along with four joint working group meetings."

The second Strategic Partnership Council meeting was held in New Delhi on 11 September 2017. Foreign Minister H.E Salahuddin Rabbani led the Afghan delegation comprising of senior members of the Afghan government. Making use of the fresh US$ one billion announced by Prime Minister, India and Afghanistan launched a new development partnership. The Government of India worked with the Government of Afghanistan to identify priorities and projects where Afghanistan needed Indian assistance to be directed. India agreed to implement some important new projects, such as the Shahtoot Dam and drinking water project for Kabul that would also facilitate irrigation, water supply for Charikar city, road connectivity to Band-e-Amir in Bamyan province that would promote tourism, low-cost housing for returning Afghan refugees in Nangarhar province to promote their resettlement, a gypsum-board-manufacturing plant in Kabul to promote value-added local industry and for import substitution, and a polyclinic in Mazar-e-Sharif.

In addition, India will also take up 116 High Impact Community Development Projects in 31 provinces of Afghanistan. These important investments will be in the areas of education, health, agriculture, irrigation, drinking water, renewable energy, flood control, micro hydropower, sports and administrative infrastructure.

India also announced that on-going programmes for education, capacity building, skills and human resource development of Afghanistan, one of the largest such programmes in the world, will continue for a further period of five years from 2017 to 2022.

Afghanistan has been an important trading and craft centre for over 2,000 years, connecting the civilisations of Persia, Central Asia with India. However, over three decades of war have undermined Afghanistan's unique tradition the last three of art and architecture. Today, the biggest challenge for Afghanistan is to rediscover and sustain its ancient art and architectural knowledge. India and Afghanistan share a centuries-old cultural heritage with deep-rooted linkages in the field of music, arts, architecture, language and cuisine.

In the field of music, in particular, most Afghan musicians were trained in the Patiala *gharana*. Today, Indian films, songs and TV serials are popular with the masses, contributing significantly to the popularisation of Hindi and familiarisation of the populace with Indian socio-cultural value system. As part of India's restructuring programme for Afghanistan, India has regularly aimed to take up projects that will render Afghanistan's cultural heritage sustainable. The Indian cultural centre has also been working towards building a shared cultural heritage."

India's engagement with Afghanistan has brought development and stability to the war-torn region. As Afghanistan matures as a democracy and seeks to develop itself, it knows that India will be there as a friend.

Unlike other nations which seek to utilise Afghanistan as an asset for its strategic location, India has deepened its cultural and economic bonds with the people of Afghanistan. The world today acknowledges the positive role played by the Modi government in stabilising a conflict-ridden region. Even in Washington, India is today an important part of its Afghan strategy.

A stable Afghanistan which has friendly relations with India is a powerful antidote to Pakistan.

Pakistan

India-Pakistan relations can be summarised using a pattern:

- India initiates a dialogue.
- Pakistan reciprocates with a terror attack.
- India suspends the dialogue and the process is repeated.

Atal Bihari Vajpayee took a bold step on assuming office. He initiated people-to-people contact, and inaugurated bus routes. He was ready to discuss all issues including that of Jammu & Kashmir. He went on a bus trip to Pakistan. Hope and enthusiasm were in the air.

Pakistan responded with the Kargil war and an attack on Indian Parliament.

Manmohan Singh as a Prime Minister not only continued back-channel dialogue started by Vajpayee but went a step further – he de-linked terror and talks. Pakistan responded by attacking Mumbai.

It is not hard to understand Pakistan's behaviour. Pakistan's identity is linked to opposing India. Even after losing many wars, it is still adventurous, wanting to measure its self-worth in its ability to stand up to India. The mere act of provoking India is perceived as a victory. Pakistan also knows that India, being the largest country in the subcontinent, can be influenced by the global community and be pressurised to make peace with smaller communities, like Pakistan.

India has also never retaliated post a terror attack and hence the risk of using non-state actors was minimal. In addition, Pakistan is always happy to lease its territory to the US or China in lieu of support against India.

Narendra Modi being a statesman did invite the Prime Minister of Pakistan for his swearing-in ceremony. He also made an unscheduled stopover at Lahore in 2015. On his way back from Kabul, Prime Minister Modi called up Nawaz Sharif and made an unplanned stop. It was the first visit by an Indian Prime Minister in 10 years. Prime Minister was bold and innovative. His move signaled to the Pakistani society that here isan Indian leader who had the courage to change India-Pakistani ties forever.

According to the Ministry of External Affairs:

"Prime Minister Narendra Modi visited Lahore on his way back from Kabul on 25 December2015. The brief stopover at Lahore was decided after the Prime Minister telephoned PMNS to convey his birthday greetings. The Prime Minister was received at the Allama Iqbal International Airport in Lahore by Prime Minister Nawaz Sharif and Punjab Chief Minister Shabaz Sharif on December 25 afternoon and flown to Pakistan PM's residence at Rawalpindi in a helicopter. Both the Prime Ministers held talks on bilateral relations. The impromptu visit to Lahore by Prime Minister Modi was generally welcomed in Pakistan."

Pakistan failed to seize the moment. It responded like it has done in the past to an invitefrom India – with a terror attack in Pathankot on 2nd January 2016. Pakistan, like always, blamed the non-state actors. Modi demanded that the non-state actors be brought to justice. Pakistan, like always, faked an inquiry which did not yield anything.

Pakistan had underestimated Narendra Modi. It had assumed that India would suspend talks only to resume then. They got a rude shock when India launched surgical strikes in Pakistan by crossing the LoC. Indian forces destroyed terror camps and returned back unharmed.

For the first time, India broke the pattern of not responding. Moreover, a clear message was sent to Rawalpindi and the ISI that India will not hesitate to cross the border if attacked.

An Indian national, Mr. Kulbhushan Jadhav was purportedly caught by Pakistani agencies under suspicious circumstances in March 2016. The High Commission of India in Islamabad has so far sent 21 notes, seeking consular access as required under the norms of the Vienna Convention on Consular Relations. However, the Government of Pakistan did not respond. The Pakistani authorities announced on 10 April 2017 that a Field General Court Martial (FGCM) awarded death sentence to Kulbhushan Jadhav under the Pakistani Army Act (PAA). Two petitions from the mother of Kulbhushan Jadhav were handed over to Pakistan's Foreign Secretary on 26 April 2017 by the High Commissioner requesting it to be filed before the Court of Appeal and the Government of Pakistan on behalf of Mr Jadhav.

Concerned over the safety of Mr Kulbhushan Jadhav, the Government of India approached the International

Court of justice (ICJ) at The Hague on 8 May 2017 against violation of Vienna Convention on Consular Relations, 1963 by Pakistan. The ICJ, in its interim ruling on 18 May 2017, has stayed the death sentence until the final decision on the proceedings. All-tough Pakistan did allow Kulbhushan Jadhav's mother and wife to meet him in captivity; many in India were concerned about the way they were treated. Doubts have also been raised on the mental and physical health of Kulbhushan Jadhav.

Modi policy on Pakistan has been clear from day one — isolate Pakistan in the region and globally engage them on India's terms and when needed, use surgical strikes to respond back in kind.

Modi has effectively engaged Afghanistan and has positioned India as a key regional player to stabilise Afghanistan. He engaged with the Arab countries to further isolate Pakistan.

Pakistan is yet to recover from the surgical strikes. Its asymmetrical use of non-state actors to wage a war against India has now been blunted. Pakistan is now struggling to make itself relevant in the region. Globally it has lost all credibility. Economically, it is now dependent on aid for survival.

This diplomatic and economic isolation of Pakistan is the biggest foreign policy achievement of the Modi government.

China

According to the Ministry of External Affairs:

"India-China cultural exchanges date back to many centuries and there is some evidence that conceptual and linguistic exchanges existed in 1500-1000 BC between the Shang-Zhou civilisation and the ancient Vedic civilisation.

During first, second and third centuries AD several Buddhist pilgrims and scholars travelled to China on the historic Silk Route. Kashyapa Matanga and Dharmaratna made the White Horse monastery at Luoyang their abode. Ancient Indian monk-scholars, such as Kumarajiva, Bodhidharma and Dharmakshema contributed to the spread of Buddhism in China. Similarly, Chinese pilgrims also undertook journeys to India, the most famous among them being Faxian and Xuanzang."

India was the first country in the non-socialist block to establish diplomatic relations with the People's Republic of China. India under Jawaharlal Nehru also aided China to secure a permanent seat at the UN Security Council. After India's defeat in the Indo-Sino war 1962, India had for decades ignored China.

China continues to make territorial claims over parts of north-east and Jammu & Kashmir. Atal Bihari Vajpayee attempted to normalise relations when he established a framework to resolve all boundary issues. India's China policy under Manmohan Singh can be best described by the title of Arun Shourie's book,'Self-Deception'.

China as a country only respects strength. The only way to deal with China is from a position of strength. To demonstrate strength requires a leader with courage. India got a Prime Minister in 2014 who proudly proclaimed that India will neither look up to or look down on any country; India will deal with every country in the world as an equal partner.

There is no better demonstration of this intent than in Modi's dealings with China. As economic growth fuelled by exports stagnates; China too needs a market for its goods. During President Xi Jingping's visit to India in 2014, the economic potential for market was showcased.

According to the Ministry of External Affairs:

"During the State visit of Chinese President Mr Xi Jinping to India from 17 to 19 September 2014, a total of 16 agreements were signed in various sectors, including commerce and trade, railways, space co-operation, pharmaceuticals, audio-visual co-production, culture, the establishment of industrial parks, sister-city arrangements, etc. The two sides also signed an MoU to open an additional route for Kailash-Mansarovar Yatra through Nathu La. The Chinese side agreed to establish two Chinese Industrial Parks in India and expressed its intention to enhance Chinese investment in India.

As President Xi Jingping's visit to India was coming to an end, reports emerged of adventurous activities of the Chinese army at the border. Prime Minister Narendra Modi in no uncertain terms communicated India's displeasure to the Chinese President.

A clear message was sent. India will deal with China as an equal stakeholder in shaping the destiny of Asia. India has now got over the hangover of the 1962 defeat.

Prime Minister Narendra Modi visited China from May 14-16, 2015. Besides meeting with the Chinese leadership, Prime Minister Modi and Premier Li also addressed the opening session of the first State/Provincial Leaders' Forum in Beijing. There were 24 agreements signed on a government-to-government basis, 26 MoUs on the business-to-business side and two joint statements, including one on climate change. Prime Minister also announced the extension of e-visa facility to Chinese nationals wishing to travel to India.

Prime Minister continued to engage China on cultural and economic fronts while clearly drawing the line on issues dealing with India's security and sovereignty.

Indian Bollywood movies were popular in China in the 1960s and 1970s and the popularity is being rekindled in recent times again. India and China have entered into an agreement on co-production of movies, the first of which based on the life of the monk Xuanzang hit the theatres in 2016.

Yoga is becoming increasingly popular in China. China was one of the co-sponsors to the UN resolution designating June 21 as the International Day of Yoga. During the visit of Prime Minister Narendra Modi to China in May 2015, a Yoga-Taichi performance in the world heritage site of Temple of Heaven was witnessed by Premier Li Keqiang and the Prime Minister. During the same visit, an agreement was signed to establish a Yoga College at Kunming, Yunnan province.

In recent events, on 20 June 2017, the eve of International Day of Yoga, a successful Yoga@Great Wall event was organised at the Juyongguan section of the Great Wall. Minister of State for External Affairs, Gen. (Dr) V.K. Singh (Retd.) attended the event.

Colours of India Festival showcasing a unique blend of Indian performing arts, Bollywood movies and Indian photography was held from 15-26 May 2017 at Beijing and Nanjing. The 2nd International Conference of Indologists, 2016 was successfully held at Shenzhen from 11-13 November 2016. The conference saw the participation of more than 75 Indologists from the world over, including China, Germany, Thailand, Chile and India. An exhibition of Gupta Art at the Palace Museum in Beijing, titled 'Across the Silk Road: Gupta Sculptures and their Chinese Counterparts, 400-700 CE' featuring 56 Indian sculptures was held in the year 2016.

In May 2017, China had organised the Belt & Road Initiative Summit in Beijing. As many as 120 countries including 29 Heads of State participated. India chose to boycott the event as the China-Pakistan Economic Corridor (CPEC) via Pakistan-occupied Kashmir challenged India's sovereignty and territorial integrity. Modi sent a clear message by not attending the went.

In June 2017, China moved into Doklam which is located in Bhutan. After threatening India with attacks for two months, China eventually reached a settlement with India to withdraw from Doklam on August 28.

On 5th September, Prime Minister Narendra Modi and President Xi Jinping held hour-long discussions on the sidelines of the BRICS summit. They agreed on a 'forward-looking' approach and vowed to make efforts to ensure that situations like the Doklam standoff do not recur. They reaffirmed that maintaining peace and tranquility in the border areas was essential for maintaining good relations between the two countries.

Modi once again proved that he is more than willing to engage with China when it comes to commerce or culture but will not give an inch when it comes to India's sovereignty, security and her role in the region.

This resolve and resilience demonstrated by the government to resolve issues with China with dignity and poise showed that India is ready to play a pivotal role at the global stage.

Prime Minister Narendra Modi again visited China in April 2018. A press release by the Ministry of External Affairs noted:

"Prime Minister Modi and President Xi believe that the simultaneous emergence of India and China as two large economies and major powers with strategic and decisional autonomy has implications of regional and global significance. They shared the view that peaceful, stable and balanced relations between India and China will be a positive factor for stability amidst current global uncertainties. They also agreed that proper management of the bilateral relationship will be conducive for the development and prosperity of the region, and will create the conditions for the Asian Century. To this end, they decided to strengthen the Closer Development Partnership in a mutually beneficial and sustainable manner, in pursuit of national modernisation and greater prosperity for their peoples."

The last four years of India's China policy has eliminated the hangover of the 1962 defeat. India is willing to engage with China as an equal. Doklam and India's handling of it clearly demonstrated that Narendra Modi's India is not the India of 1962 under Jawaharlal Nehru. In 1962, we failed at diplomacy and war. In 2018, we used diplomacy to avert a war.

❐

2

India and US – Natural Allies

"Today, at 15:45 hours, India conducted three underground nuclear tests in the Pokhran range. The tests conducted today were with a fission device, a low-yield device and a thermonuclear device. The measured yields are in line with expected values. Measurements have also confirmed that there was no release of radioactivity into the atmosphere. There were contained explosions like the experiment conducted in May 1974. I warmly congratulate the scientists and engineers who have carried out these successful tests."

Atal Bihari Vajpayee, 13 May 1998

India's nuclear tests of 1998 severely strained India-US relations. The US not only strongly condemned India's actions but also imposed economic sanctions. The US intelligence community was also embarrassed as they had no clue on India's intent to conduct tests. This failure of the US community was described as the 'intelligence failure of the decade'.

The sanctions on India cut off all assistance to India except humanitarian aid, banning the export of certain Defence material and technologies, ending American credit and credit guarantees to India, and requiring the US to oppose lending by international financial institutions to India.

Many believed that India would find it hard to recover from the sanctions and would need to give up her nuclear ambitions for survival. Actions from the US were followed by other countries, such as Canada, Japan and Australia. The NDA government under Atal Bihari Vajpayee moved swiftly to re-cast India-US ties.

Atal Bihari Vajpayee chose to re-build India-US relations on the foundation of democracy and shared values. Over the next five years, not only were sanctions lifted but a framework was established that would recognise India as a responsible nuclear power.

When Manmohan Singh took office, India-US ties were strong. From imposing sanctions in 1998, the US was now eager to offer a civil nuclear deal to India. The US was ready to engage with India and elevate the India-US relationship to a strategic partnership based on the foundation outlined by Atal Bihari Vajpayee.

Manmohan Singh's government, which was supported by the Communist Party of India, was under pressure to distance itself from the US. For UPA-1 government, US was an imperialist country to be wary of and not an ally with whom you could have a strategic partnership. Manmohan Singh put his own personal credibility at stake and managed to sign the India-US nuclear deal. Little did he know that his allies would never allow him to implement the deal.

India-US relations soon became dormant. The US found that India could not deliver on her own promises. Even the word of the Prime Minister of India was not potent enough to result in action on the ground. In India too, the Nehruvian legacy of non-alignment re-surfaced. It was prudent to keep an arm's length from an imperialist power, like the US. The US was no doubt very disappointed in the lack of initiative and interest shown by India to elevate and deepen the partnership.

After Modi's landslide win in the 2014 elections, the US administration was not very sure on how to engage with him. As a Chief Minister of Gujarat, Modi had been unfairly denied a visa to visit the United States. One would assume that after such treatment, any leader would think twice before engaging with the US.

Narendra Modi as always put the national interest first and accepted President Barack Obama's invitation to visit the US in September 2014.

Modi's first task as a Prime Minister was to rejuvenate the dormant ties with the US. So he started from where Atal Bihari Vajpayee had left. He articulated that India and US are natural allies as two of the largest democracies in the world.

Modi's first visit to the US also demonstrated some innovative diplomacy – economic diplomacy and leveraging the large US diaspora as cultural ambassadors to further India's cause.

Two days before stepping foot in the White House to meet Obama, Modi addressed Indian Americans at the Madison Square Garden.

The New York Times covered the event and reported

"They wore his face on their chests, waved it on posters, chanted his name and quoted his slogans; 19,000 fans drawn to a single star. His image stared down from the big screen at Madison Square Garden and emerged on canvas in a live speed-painting onstage. And when the man himself emerged, the capacity crowd on Sunday in New York's most storied arena roared as one, as if all the Knicks, all the Rangers, Billy Joel and Bruce Springsteen had suddenly materialised."

"His hero's welcome must have seemed slightly stunning

to the three dozen or so American elected officials who turned up to greet him, including several senators, 30-odd representatives and one Governor, each of whom strode onstage to no more than polite applause."

"His speech, when it came, did not disappoint. Casting himself as a man of humble origins with 'the intention to do big things for small people,' he vowed to promote Indian economic growth, clean up the polluted Ganges river and improve the lot of the country's poor and disadvantaged. He promised to make it easier for those of Indian descent to obtain visas, so that members of the Indian diaspora might bring their talents back to the homeland."

A poor tea-seller from India banned from visiting the US for a decade had done what any American rock star can only dream of – fill Madison Square Garden and get a roaring welcome in front of 30-odd Senators/Governors.

Modi also reached out to the captains of the US commerce and industry, the American civil society and think tanks. The focus of these meetings was economic diplomacy, i.e. make it easy for US companies to invest and make in India. Modi also highlighted India's demographic dividend and the demand from this young market which would make India one of the most attractive markets in the world for goods and services.

As Narendra Modi walked into the White House to be received by President Obama, the American administration experienced first hand that they were dealing with a strong, popular leader who was supported not only back home, but even by the Indian community in America.

Modi used his first meeting with President Obama to elevate Indo-US relations to a 'global strategic partnership'. A Vision Statement and a Joint Statement were issued during the visit. A rare joint op-ed was penned by Prime Minister Narendra Modi and President Obama for *Washington Post*.

A few quotes from the op-ed beautifully describe the strategic nature of the India-US relations that was outlined by the two leaders:

"India and the United States are bound by common values and mutual interests. We have each shaped the positive trajectory of human history, and through our joint efforts, our natural and unique partnership can help shape international security and peace for years to come."

"The true potential of our relationship has yet to be fully realised. The advent of a new government in India is a natural opportunity to broaden and deepen our relationship. ...It is time to set a new agenda — one that realises concrete benefits for our citizens."

"This will be an agenda that enables us to find mutually rewarding ways to expand our collaboration in trade, investment and technology that harmonise with India's ambitious development agendawhile sustaining the United States as the global engine of growth."

"We will discuss ways in which our businesses, scientists and governments can partner... an immediate area of concrete support is the 'Clean India' campaign, where we will leverage private and civil society innovation, expertise and technology to improve sanitation and hygiene throughout India."

The promise of a better tomorrow is not solely for Indians and Americans: It also beckons us to move forward together for a better world. This is the central premise of our defining partnership for the 21st century. Forward together we go — *chalein saath saath*."

India-US partnership has only grown since 2014. According to the Ministry of External Affairs:

"President Obama's visit to India on 25-27 January 2015 as the Chief Guest at India's Republic Day — during the visit, the two sides issued a Delhi Declaration of Friendship and adopted a Joint Strategic Vision for Asia-Pacific and the Indian Ocean region. Both sides elevated the Strategic Dialogue between their Foreign Ministers to Strategic and Commercial Dialogue of Foreign and Commerce Ministers."

A key highlight of this visit was President Barck Obama joining Prime Minister Narendra Modi in his hugely popular 'Mann Ki Baat' programme. Narendra Modi has always been very innovative and creative in building a personal connection with global leaders. This was another example of how the personal chemistry between leaders accelerated bilateral relations between two countries.

Prime Minister Modi again visited the US on 23-28 September 2015, during which he held a bilateral meeting with President Obama, interacted with leaders of business, media, academia, the provincial leaders and the Indian community, during his travel to the Silicon Valley. In 2016, Prime Minister visited the US for the multilateral Nuclear Security Summit hosted by President Obama in Washington DC on 31 March-1 April. This was soon followed by an official working visit by Prime Minister on 6-8 June, during which he held bilateral discussions with President Obama, and also addressed a joint session of the US Congress. Prime Minister Modi was the sixth Indian Prime Minister to address the US Congress.

There is a frequent interaction between the leadership of the two countries, including telephone calls and meetings on the sidelines of international summits. A hotline has been established between the Prime Minister's Office and the US White House.

During the visit of Prime Minister to the US in June 2016, the US recognised India as a 'Major Defence Partner', which commits the US to facilitate technology sharing with India to a level commensurate with that of its closest allies and partners, and industry collaboration for Defence co-production and co-development.

India and the US, an arrangement was concluded in June 2016 to facilitate the exchange of terrorist screening information through the designated contact points. India-US Joint Working Group on Counter-Terrorism held its 14th meeting in July 2016 in Washington DC."

Modi's personal involvement in elevating India-US ties to a level of strategic partnership has been remarkable. Prime Minister Modi has truly lived up to his party's commitment of 'Nation First, Self Last'. India today is not only a strategic partner but also a critical ally in maintaining geo-political balance in the region.

❒

3
Japan — A 1,400-Year-old Friendship

India's relations with Japan is more than 1,400 years old. In 752 AD, Bodhisena, an Indian monk performed the eye-opening ceremony of the Buddha statue at the Todaiji temple. There has never been a conflict between India and Japan over the last 1,400 years. Relations between India and Japan are that of mutualrespect.

Swami Vivekananda had once remarked, "I would wish that everyone of our young men could visit Japan once at least in his lifetime." Swami Vivekananda admired the patriotism and art of Japan. Subhas Chandra Bose too found an ally in Japan who provided significant support to build the Indian National Army.

Post World War II, at the Tokyo War Crimes Tribunal, Justice Radhabinod Pal became famous for his dissenting judgement in favour of Japan. The judgement of Justice Radhabinod Pal is remembered even today in Japan. This became a symbol of the close ties between India and Japan.

However, post-independence, the momentum of ties between the two countries significantly slowed down. After Prime Minister Hayato Ikeda's visit to India in 1961, the next prime ministerial visit from Japan was by Yasuhiro Nakasone in 1984. However, despite this, Japan continued to be an ally of India. Japan played a pivotal role in revolutionising the automotive industry in India with the launch of Maruti-Suzuki card in India. Japan is also one of the very few countries in the world to unconditionally support India during the 1991 monetary crisis.

Prime Minister Manmohan Singh elevated India-Japan relations to a 'strategic partnership'. Prime Minister Narendra Modi went a step further.

As reported by the Ministry of Foreign Affairs:

"Prime Minister Shri Narendra Modi visited Japan from 30 August to 3 September2014 for the 9th Annual Summit Meeting with Prime Minister Shinzo Abe. During the visit, the two sides upgraded the relationship to a 'Special Strategic and Global Partnership'. Both sides also agreed to establish the 'India-Japan Investment Promotion Partnership'. Prime Minister Abe pledged to realise public and private investments worth yen 3.5 trillion and doubling of the number of Japanese companies in India over the next five years.

"Prime Minister Shinzo Abe visited India for the 10th Annual Summit with Prime Minister Shri Narendra Modi from 11-13 December 2015. As many as 16 agreements/MoUs/MoCs/LoIs were signed/exchanged during the visit. In a special gesture, India also announced 'visa on arrival' scheme to all Japanese travellers, including for business purposes, from 1st March2016. Prime Minister Abe, accompanied by Prime Minister Modi also visited the city of Varanasi, which signed a partnership agreement with the city of Kyoto in August 2014. A 'Japan-India Make in India Special Finance Facility' of JPY 1.3 trillion was also established.

"Prime Minister Narendra Modi visited Japan for the 11th

Annual Summit from 10-12 November 2016. Following their meeting, the two Prime Ministers issued a joint statement and a fact sheet. Nearly 10 agreements/MoUs/MoCs were signed/exchanged in a wide range of areas, including co-operation in peaceful uses of nuclear energy, manufacturing skill transfer programme, outer space, marine, earth and atmospheric science and technology, agriculture and food-related industry, transport and urban development, textiles, cultural exchange and sports. Prime Minister Modi travelled on the shinkansen, accompanied by Prime Minister Abe to Kobe, where a MoU between the state of Gujarat and Hyogo Prefecture was signed."

India is not a signatory to the Non-Proliferation Treaty (NPT), and is the only non-signatory to receive an exemption from Japan. The two sides also signed agreements on manufacturing skill development in India, co-operation in space, earth sciences, agriculture, forestry and fisheries, transport and urban development.

Japan is the fourth largest foreign investor in India. The amount of Japan's cumulative investment in India from April 2000 to September 2016 is US$ 23.76 billion, which is nearly 8 per cent of India's overall FDI during this period. Japanese FDI into India has mainly been in automobile, electrical equipment, telecommunications, chemical and pharmaceutical sectors.

In 2017, Japan-India Coordination Forum (JICF) for Development of North-Eastern Region was announced. JICF is a coordination forum to identify priority development areas of co-operation for the development of northeast India.

Japan has also agreed to provide a 50-year loan at 0.1 per cent to build the Ahmedabad-Mumbai bullet-train link. The project was initiated in 2017 and the bullet train is expected to be completed by 2022.

During the last four years, India's 1400-year-old tieswith Japan have only become stronger. The cultural and spiritual bonds which have endured for more than 1,400 years have only got stronger.

❐

4
From 'Look East' to 'Act East'

Association of South-East Asian Nations (ASEAN) comprises of Indonesia, Singapore, Philippines, Malaysia, Brunei, Thailand, Cambodia, Laos PDR, Myanmar and Vietnam.

India and the ASEAN countries have had strong cultural, civilisational and commercial bonds for centuries.

For many decades post-Independence, India had failed to build on centuries of relations with the ASEAN countries. India under Nehru carried forward the British legacy of being focused on the immediate neighbourhood. Neither commerce nor culture with the ASEAN countries was emphasised under Jawaharlal Nehru.

Frederic Grare, non-resident Senior Fellow, South Asia Programme, Carnegie Endowment for International Peace and author of India Turns East: International Engagement and *U.S.-China Rivalry* has summarised how ASEAN countries felt about India:

"There has been occasional frustration and ASEAN members, at least the most important of them, seem to believe that India constantly plays below its weight category and so they often complain about India's insufficient assertiveness in ASEAN's activities."

In the 1990s, things changed for the better when

following the launch of India's 'Look East Policy', Modi transformed India's ASEAN policy from 'Look East' to ' Act East'. India has also set up a separate mission to ASEAN and the EAS in Jakarta in April 2015 with a dedicated Ambassador to strengthen engagement with ASEAN and ASEAN-centric processes.

The key principles of Modi's 'Act East Policy' are:

- **Connectivity:** Better transport connectivity is critical to India-ASEAN relations. After all, the seamless movement of goods and services across borders is highly dependent on effective transportation links. To deepen connectivity between India and ASEAN nations, it is essential to build effective institutional connectivity by harmonising trade, investments and financial policies. People-to-people connectivity can be improved by enabling the movement of citizens.
- **Commerce:** With connectivity, India can easily integrate with the ASEAN. A large economic bloc would accelerate the growth of ASEAN as well as India.
- **Culture:** At the 31st ASEAN Summit held in Manila, a musical version of *Ramayana* was performed at the opening ceremony. *Ramayana* was chosen as it is an integral part of the history and culture of ASEAN nations. This shared history with India creates a timeless bond between India and ASEAN. The Modi Government has integrated culture as a part of his 'Act East Policy'.

More than connectivity, commerce or culture, ASEAN is looking for an ally who can provide peace and security in the region. China has long pending disputes with many of the ASEAN countries. China has also refused to abide by any decisions of the international courts on these disputes.

India has the potential to step in as a stabilising and

balancing force which can provide peace and prosperity to the ASEAN region. In Modi, the ASEAN leaders have found a leader they can count on.

26 January 2018 was a historical day for India-ASEAN relations. All the Heads of State of the 10 ASEAN countries participated as chief guests at India's Republic Day celebrations.

When connectivity issues are resolved, culture and commerce tend to take over. The mixture of culture and commerce will create a strong, sustainable bond between India and ASEAN.

Modi's 'Act East' policy will change the geo-politics of the region. It will also be his enduring legacy for decades to come.

❐

5
Australia – Ties that Bind

Australia's relations with India have been transformed since Modi assumed office in 2014. From condemning India in 1998 for the nuclear tests to signing the nuclear deal with India in 2014, the relationship has transcended engagements which were earlier limited to commerce and sport.

A Civil Nuclear Co-operation Agreement between the two countries was signed in September 2014 during the visit of the then Prime Minister Tony Abbott to India. The agreement came into force from 13 November 2015 and provides the framework for substantial new trade in energy between Australia and India. The Australian Parliament passed the 'Civil Nuclear Transfer to India Bill 2016' on 1 December, 2016 which ensures that uranium mining companies in Australia may fulfil contracts to supply Australian uranium to India for civil use with the confidence that exports would not be hindered by domestic legal action challenging the consistency of the safeguards applied by the IAEA in India and Australia's international non-proliferation obligations. It also ensures that any future bilateral trade in other nuclear-related material or items for civil use will also be protected.

During Prime Minister Modi's visit to Australia in

November 2014, both sides decided to extend Defence co-operation to cover research, development and industry engagement. They agreed to hold regular meetings at the level of the Defence Minister, conduct regular maritime exercises and convene regular service-to-service talks. As a result, the then Australian Defence Minister, Mr Kevin Andrews, visited India during 1-3 September 2015 for bilateral talks, including issues related to security co-operation with then Raksha Mantri Manohar Parrikar. Our CNS Admiral, R.K. Dhowan visited Australia during 2-7 October 2015 for bilateral talks, attended Sea Power Conference 2015 in Sydney and signed a technical agreement on White Shipping Information Exchange.

An Australia-India Strategic Research Fund (AISRF) has been set up; the two countries have identified a number of collaborative research projects in areas such as agricultural research, astronomy and astrophysics, environmental sciences, microelectronics, nanotechnology, renewable energy, marine sciences and earth systems sciences. The tenth anniversary of the AISRF was celebrated during the recent visit of Australian Prime Minister Turnbull to India.

The fund, where each side contributed A$ 65 million over a five-year period, supports large-scale research projects designed to deliver practical solutions, focusingon energy, food and water security, health and the environment. AISRF consists of India-Australia Biotechnology Fund, India-Australia Science & Technology Fund, Grand Challenge Fund and Fellowship Schemes. Joint committees on S&T and biotechnology have been established to administer the fund. The Australian side is also co-operating in our Clean Ganga Project as agreed during the visit of our Prime Minister to Australia in 2014. Secretary (Water Resources, River

Development and Ganga Rejuvenation) led a delegation to Australia during 19-25 the June 2016 for bilateral co-operation on water resource management, including discussion on Ganga rejuvenation.

During her visit to India in July 2017, Foreign Minister Ms Julie Bishop signed a framework agreement for Australia to join the International Solar Alliance, led by the Governments of India and France.

Australia has also agreed to help in establishing a Sports University in India. Secretary (Sports) Rajiv Yadav led a delegation to Australia during 7-11 October 2016 for study and discussion with Australian Sports University for setting up a National Sports University in India. A MoU on cooperation in sports was signed during the visit of Prime Minister Turnbull to India in April 2017. A MoU in the field of tourism was signed between the two countries during the visit of Prime Minister Modi to Australia in November 2014, which is expected to promote and support the growth in the tourism industry.

Australia along with Japan and India has also set up a trilateral dialogue. Maritime security was on the agenda, including freedom of navigation in the South China Sea and trilateral maritime co-operation in the Indian Ocean and the Pacific Ocean. The countries also discussed the prospects for greater economic co-operation.

Australian Prime Minister Malcolm Turnbull, during his visit to India in 2017, hailed Prime Minister Narendra Modi for "leading this most remarkable nation (India) on an extraordinary journey of growth and development." Heaping praise on Prime Minister Modi, Turnbull said, "A achievements of India are the admiration of the world."

He also underlined, "We look forward to working even

more closely than we have done in past." Turnbull was accorded a ceremonial reception at the President House. "We are bound together to ties of history of values of people. We look forward, Prime Minister (Modi) and I, to making that even stronger in this visit," Turnbull added.

Highlight of Malcolm Trunbull's visit was a visit to the Swaminarayan Temple in Delhi along with Modi.

With strategic partnerships with Australia and Japan, India has not only secured her interests in the region but has also got over its colonial hangover of limiting her influence to the South Asia region. India with her deep strategic relationships with Australia, Japan and ASEAN has emerged as an important player in Asia-Pacific.

❐

6
Not Shy about Israel

India and Israel have a lot in common. Both countries became independent around the same time from British. Both India and Israel are surrounded by countries which fund and train terrorists. Both have been victims of terror.

However, post-independence, India and Israel went separate ways. India chose to isolate her economy and remained non-aligned, Israel integrated its economy with the Western world.

Source: mea.gov.in

Till 2014, India did establish formal relations with Israel and co-operated on Defence and security, India was always shy of acknowledging its relations with Israel. Politicians in India feared that if they would acknowledge or upgrade relations with Israel, they would lose the support of the large Muslim population in India. Communal vote bank politics took precedence over alliance with Israel. No Prime Minister dared to visit Israel for the fear of losing Muslim votes.

All this changed with the election of Modi in 2014. As reported by the Jewish Virtual Library:

"India-Israel co-operation increased dramatically in 2014 with the election of India's new Prime Minister, Narendra Modi. Between Modi's election in May 2014 and November 2014, Israel exported $662 million worth of Israeli weapons and Defence items to India. This export number is greater than the total Israeli exports to India during the previous three years combined. Israeli Defence Minister Moshe Ya'alon made the first ever official visit as an Israeli Defence Minister to India in February 2015. While in India, Ya'alon, along with many other top Israeli defence officials, attended the Aero India Arms Exhibition in Bangalore. The purpose of Ya'alon's trip was to increase interaction and co-operation between Defence industries in Israel and India. Photos surfaced online the following day of Indian Prime Minister Narendra Modi standing at the Israel Aerospace Industries booth at the exhibition, in a public display of Israel's and India's strategic relationship."

Israel Aerospace Industries successfully tested a jointly developed Indian-Israeli Barak-8 air and naval Defence missile system on 10 November 2014. The missile test was carried out by Israel's Defence Ministry and India's Defence Research and Development Organisation and represents the first fully successful test of the missile. A top advisor to India's Defence Minister hailed the test as "an important milestone in co-operation between India and Israel."

Israel Aerospace Industries (IAI) and the Indian state-owned Defence Research and Development Organisation (DRDO) began collaborating on a jointly developed surface-to-air missile system for the Indian Army in 2015. Indian officials purchased 321 launchers and 8,356 missiles from the Israeli military in 2015. India uses Israel-made unmanned drones for surveillance and military purposes, and ordered 16 drones during 2015.

The Government of India quietly approved the purchase of 10 armored Heron TP drone vehicles from Israel on 11 September 2015, at a price of $400 million. These drones will help secure India's borders and will be operated by members of India's Air Force. An original proposal for the purchase was presented in 2012, but the programme did not receive political backing until 2015.

The Barak-8 long-range surface-to-air missile, developed jointly by India and Israel, was successfully tested on 30th December 2015. The test of the missile system, which cost the Indian government approximately $1.4 billion, was carried out on the Indian warship *'INS Kolkata'*. India again successfully tested the Barak-8 on 30 June 2016. An Indian Defence official praised the test, stating "The test launch was a grand success and it met all the targets." The Barak-8 was developed by India's Defence Research and Development Organisation in collaboration with Israel Aerospace Industries and can be launched from a ship or from land. Another successful test of the Barak-8 missile was carried out on 20 September 2016, at the Chandipur research and development base in Odisha, on the Bay of Bengal.

Indian firm Reliance Defence and Israeli firm Rafael Advanced Defence Systems signed a co-operation agreement worth an estimated $10 billion at Defexpo India on 30 March

2016. A per the agreement, Rafael and Reliance will co-operatively produce air-to-air missiles, various missile defence systems and surveillance balloons for the Indian military. The undertaking is projected to provide employment to 3,000 Indians at a facility in the Indian state of Madhya Pradesh.

The Indian Navy launched a new, Israeli-developed Integrated Under Water Harbour Defence and Surveillance System (IUHDSS), in February 2017. The system will enhance the security of above-and below-water vehicles operated by the Indian Navy in the Mumbai naval harbour.

In October 2014 India and Israel reached a deal for India to purchase 8,356 Spike anti-tank guided missiles and 321 missile launchers developed by Israeli Rafael Advanced Defence Systems Ltd. This contract was deferred prior to its signature, howeverdue to costs and vendor issues. The Indian Ministry of Defence announced in March 2017 that the contract, worth approximately $1 billion, would finally be moving forward.

Israel Aerospace Industries (IAI) announced in April 2017 that it had struck a deal with India's Army and Navy to supply them with an advanced air defence system worth upwards of $2 billion. The deal was described by IAI as Israel's largest ever Defence deal.

On 10 May 2017, three warships from the Indian Navy docked in the port of Haifa, ahead of Indian Prime Minister Modi's scheduled visit during the summer. The ships, the 'INS Mumbai', the 'INS Trishul', and the 'INS Aditya', participated in a naval drill with the Israeli Navy when they entered the port. This is the eighth time that Indian ships have docked at an Israeli port, the first being in 2000.

The Indian military carried out their first successful tests of the Israeli-made surface-to-air Python and Derby missile system (SPYDER) on 11 May 2017. The launch of the SPYDER system went off without a hitch and all three missiles that were launched hit their targets. Python and Derby missile comprise the SPYDER system, which also features an onboard radar for increased accuracy. The system, which is made for low-altitude missile strikes, has a range of 15 km.

A new partnership between Indian security firm Punj Lloyd and Israel Weapons Industries, known as Punj Lloyd Raksha Systems, or PLR, was announced in May 2017. The firm produces small arms from the Israel Weapons Industries product line and is the first private small-arms manufacturer in India to produce equipment for both local and export use. Ashok Wadhawan, the president of manufacturing at Punj Lloyd, explained that the joint venture aims to target the supply of carbine, assault rifle, sniper rifle and light machine guns for armed forces, paramilitary forces and state police.

Indian Prime Minister Modi's security service recruited 30 dogs from Israel in 2017, trained to attack, sniff for bombs and drugs and track criminals.

The Indian military deployed an Israeli-developed Comprehensive Integrated Border Management System (CIBMS) along its border with Pakistan in August 2017. The fence will be monitored by sensors and security cameras and will alert people in monitoring facilities when a breach has occurred. Indian officials announced plans to seal their 6,300 km borders with Pakistan and Bangladesh with the Israeli smart-fence.

India participated in the Israeli Blue Flag military exercise for the first time in November 2017

In what was hailed as a 'huge development for India' by local news agencies, India abstained from a vote at the UNHRC that approved their Gaza Commission of Inquiry report, in July 2015. Forty-one countries voted in favour of adopting the findings of the biased report, and India was one of only five others who abstained. This marked the first time that India had ever voted against Palestinian interests at the UNHRC, signalling a significant shift in India-Israel relations.

India's ambassador to Israel, Jaideep Sarkar, encouraged the approximately 85,000 Israeli Jews of Indian descent to tour their country of origin in August 2015, amid warming ties between the nations. Sarkar stated, "We want to tell the world proudly about the rich Jewish life in India. With your efforts, we are working to preserve the Jewish heritage in India. We hope to have a package tour to Jewish heritage sites in Mumbai and elsewhere by early next year." He also suggested that these Indian-Israeli Jews should consider enrolling in higher education courses at Indian universities.

During a three-day visit to Israel in January 2016, Indian Minister of External Affairs Sushma Swaraj stated that the full development of positive Israel-India ties is of 'the highest importance,' to the Government in India.

The number of tourists from India increased dramatically from 2014 to 2015, with 40,000 Indian nationals vacationing in Israel in 2015 compared to 34,900 in 2014.

In the first visit of its kind in 20 years, Israeli President Reuven Rivlin visited India for a week in mid-November 2016. Rivlin and Indian Prime Minister Narendra Modi held discussions and meetings pertaining to security co-operation and combatting terrorism and also discussed the future of Israeli investment in India. While in India, the Israeli President also visited the Taj Mahal and observed Indian water-treatment facilities. Indian officials signed contracts worth a combined $1.4 billion with Israeli Aerospace Industries (IAI) during Rivlin's visit, on 16 November2016.

The two Defence contracts provide for the Indian purchase from Israel of two Phalcon/IL-76 Airborne Early Warning and Control Systems (AWACS), valued at $1 billion, as well as 10 additional Heron TP UAV drones, valued at $400 million.

The week before Modi's historic visit to Israel, Benjamin Netanyahu's cabinet approved measures aimed to strengthen the Israel-India relationship. During their meeting on 25 June 2017, the Israeli cabinet agreed to the adoption of measures to increase Israel's non-diamond exports to India by 25 per cent and established a new $40 million joint innovation, research and development fund. The resolutions approved also included incentives to film Bollywood movies in Israel and plan to increase the number of Indian firms doing business in Israel.

Indian Prime Minister Modi became the first sitting Indian Prime Minister to visit Israel on 4 July 2017. Israeli Prime Minister Netanyahu appeared with Modi throughout his three-day visit, accompanying him on visits to Yad Vashem and water desalination plants as well as various cultural events. Officials at the Israeli Foreign Ministry emphasised that Netanyahu's level of participation in the visit was not at all a standard and underscored the crucial importance of the trip. During Modi's trip, he did not meet with any Palestinian officials, although he met with Mahmoud Abbas in India two months prior.

Multiple collaborative agreements were signed between Indian and Israeli entities during Modi's visit. The Israel Space Agency and the Indian Space Research Organisation signed an agreement to foster partnership in the development of electric propulsion systems for small satellites and creating systems to accurately measure the extreme conditions of outer space. Israeli officials and their Indian counterparts signed an agreement to create the India-Israel Innovation Initiative

Fund (I4F) on 5 July 2017, modelled after the US-Israel BIRD Foundation. The two countries pledged $4 million per year each to I4F over a five-year period. Representatives from a number of India's largest corporations signed eight trade agreements with Israeli firms including Elbit Systems and Israel Aerospace Industries on 6 June 2017. A collaborative agreement was also signed during Modi's visit to Israel between the Asher Space Research Institute at the Technion and the Indian Institute of Space Science and Technology. This agreement aims to establish joint study and research exchange programmes.

Concluding his visit, Modi bid farewell to the people of Israel via a Twitter post in Hebrew and English that read: "I thank the people and Government of Israel for their hospitality. This successful visit will add more energy to India-Israel relations." Israeli Prime Minister Netanyahu posted a message on Twitter in Hindi language as well.

The Israeli National Emergency Medical Service, MDA-Magen David Adom (Hebrew for Red Star of David) and the Indian Red Cross Society (IRCS), held a joint training programme during July 2017 aimed at improving and upgrading the IRCS first-responder skills. "Trainers from the MDA worked with IRCS volunteers, teaching them to provide first-aid during emergencies, natural disasters and accidents and teach life-saving skills that will save precious lives," said the Director of the IRCS Blood Bank. IRCS trainees were taught the laws of first-aid and how to handle patients, in addition to how to bandage wounds, stop the flow of blood from an injury, and perform CPR on adults and children.

Narendra Modi has ensured that India has a strong partner which she can count on, be it for security or economy. ❐

7
Link West Policy

The region referred to by world as 'Middle East' is termed as 'West Asia' by India. West Asia plays a critical role in the development of India. India is dependent on West Asia to meet its energy needs. Millions of Indians reside in the region for employment. The remittances sent back by the Indians in West Asia not only boost India's forex reserves but is also critical to the economy of states, like Kerala.

Given the importance of the region, the Modi government has outlined its Link West policy. Key tenets of the Link West policy are:

Given the importance of the region, the Modi government has outlined its Link West policy. Key tenets of the Link West policy are:

- **'De-hyphenation':** Establish strong bilateral relationships with every country and not get distracted by conflicts within the region.
- **Energy Security:** Ensure India's energy security.
- **Diaspora Connect:** Engage the diaspora and use diplomacy to provide relief to the Indians in West Asia when in need.

UAE

Narendra Modi is the first Prime Minister to visit the UAE

in 34 years. According to the Ministry of External Affairs:

"Narendra Modi's visit marked the beginning of a new comprehensive and strategic partnership. In the joint statement issued after the visit, both the leaders agreed to work together not only to consolidate achievements in the existing domains, but also to explore newer areas of co-operation. H.H. Sheikh Mohamed bin Zayed Al Nahyan, Crown Prince of Abu Dhabi and Deputy Supreme Commander of UAE Armed Forces, visited India from 10-12 February, 2016 on a State visit and had wide-ranging discussions on bilateral, regional and multilateral issues of mutual interest and reached a broad consensus and signed MoUs/agreements pertaining to (i) facilitation of institutional investors in infrastructure, (ii) co-operation in renewable energy, (iii) co-operation in combating cyber-crimes, (iv) cultural exchange, (v) space, (vi) skill development, (vii) insurance and (viii) currency swaps. This was followed by his another visit to India from 24-26 January 2017 as the Chief Guest at India's Republic Day celebrations."

UAE has pledged to invest $75 Billion in India. Under Modi, relations between India and UAE have grown beyond that of a buyer and seller to a deeper partnership that focusses on investment and joint ventures in petrochemical complexes and co-operation in joint exploration in India, the UAE and in third countries.

Prime Minister Modi in February 2018 inaugurated the project for the first Hindu temple to be built in UAE capital, Abu Dhabiwhile launching the Bochasanwasi Shri Akshar Purushottam Swaminarayan Sanstha (BAPS) temple project via video conference,

Narendra Modi said, "I believe this temple will not be only unique in terms of architecture and splendour, but will also give a message of *vasudhaiva kutumbakam* to people across the world."

Saudi Arabia

India's relations with Saudi Arabia were often strained due to Saudi Arabia's support to Pakistan during wars with India and over the Kashmir issue. The emergence of India as the fastest growing market and the discovery of shale gas globally has increased the importance of India.

According to the Ministry of External Affairs:

"The visit of Prime Minister Narendra Modi to Riyadh from 2-3 April 2016 could be seen as a turning point in our growing engagement with the kingdom of Saudi Arabia, which has taken an upward strategic direction."

"PM Modi and King underlined the close and friendly bilateral ties and deep-rooted shared history between two nations. Both the leaders discussed ways to increase people-to-people ties. Both the leaders also emphasised on furthering bilateral strategic engagement in the areas of security and Defence co-operation. Also, both the nations agreed to enhance co-operation to strengthen maritime security in the Gulf and the Indian Ocean regions. Both the nations also decided to strengthen co-operation in combating terrorism both at the bilateral level and within multilateral system of the UN. King Salman Bin Abdulaziz lauded PM Modi's #StartUpIndia, #MakeInIndia, #SmartCities and #SwachhBharat initiatives. PM Modi exhorted Saudi industries to invest in India. Meanwhile, Saudi Arabia expressed keen interest in railways, roads, ports and shipping sectors in India."

In a special gesture, King Salman honoured Prime Minister Modi with the sash of King Abdulaziz, the highest civilian decoration awarded by the kingdom

Iran

India-Iran relations go back a few millennia. The two countries shared a border till 1947 apart from several common features in their language, culture and traditions

According to a BBC World Service poll conducted at the end of 2005, 71 per cent of Iranians viewed India's influence positively, with 21 per cent viewing it negatively, the most favourable rating of India for any country in the world.

On 22 May 2016, Prime Minister Modi paid an official visit to Iran. As reported by the Ministry of External Affairs:

"Prime Minister Narendra Modi paid a bilateral visit to Iran from 22-23 May 2016. 12 MoUs/agreements were signed between India and Iran. A trilateral agreement on transit and transport was signed between India, Iran and Afghanistan in the presence of Prime Minister Modi, President Rouhani and Afghan President Ashraf Ghani. Prime Minister Modi also inaugurated the international conference titled 'India-Iran, Two Great Civilisations' in Vahdat Hall, Tehran and Prime Minister Modi released a Persian manuscript *Kalileh Wa Dimneh*."

Iranian President Hassan Rouhani visited India in 2018. India and Iran's relations received a boost with the signing of dozen pacts including one on double taxation avoidance and another for the leasing by an Indian company of a container terminal facility in Iran's strategically located Chabahar port.

Growing connectivity and commerce with Iran to ensure energy security for India has been a significant achievement of the Modi government.

Oman

Prime Minister Modi's visit to Oman in 2018 resulted in enhancing India's Defence ties with Oman. India managed to secure access to the strategically located Duqm port and dry dock for maintenance of Indian military vessels.

Source: mea.gov.in

Modi "welcomed the invitation to Indian companies to invest in various sectors in the special economic zones of Oman, including SEZs in Duqm, Sohar and Salalah. The Indian Prime Minister offered India's partnership and co-operation in areas of priority, such as minerals and mining, manufacturing, logistics, infrastructure, tourism, agriculture and fisheries, IT and IT-enabled services, skill development and innovation."

The Omani side acknowledged the opportunities offered under the 'Make in India' initiative for joint production of Defence equipment in India and also for the procurement of Defence material from India.

The two sides agreed to enhance co-operation to strengthen maritime security in the Gulf and the Indian

Ocean regions, vital for the security and prosperity of both the countries. They further agreed to promote bilateral collaboration for humanitarian assistance and evacuation in natural disasters and conflict situations. The Indian Prime Minister thanked His Majesty the Sultan for the Omani assistance during 'Operation Rahat' conducted by India to evacuate Indian and foreign nationals from Yemen in March-April 2015.

Prime Minister also addressed the Indian community from the royal box in Sultan Qaboos sports complex. The royal box is used only by Sultan of Oman Qaboos bin Said al Said and PM was the first visiting dignitary who was given the honour of addressing the community from there.

❐

8
New Momentum to Ties with Europe

Diplomatic relations with Europe acquired a new momentum under the Narendra Modi government with a spate of high-level visits from both sides. For the first time in decades,we saw the Indian Prime Minister visiting many European countries.

Many European countries have actively invested in development programmes in India, such as #MakeInIndia, Skill Development, Digital India and *Namami Gange*. India and Europe also saw greater co-operation in areas of counter-terrorism and cybersecurity.

United Kingdom

Prime Minister Modi's visit to the UK from 12-14 November 2015 took the relationship between the largest democracy and the oldest democracy to new heights.

A press release by the mea.gov.in noted that:

"During the visit, the two Prime Ministers endorsed a vision statement setting out the fundamental principles on which UK-India partnership is built and outlined a roadmap for deepening co-operation. Both Prime Ministers resolved to hold biennial PM-level summits to advance the partnership and agreed on a new Defence and International Security

Partnership aimed to intensify co-operation in Defence and security, including cybersecurity, counter-terrorism and maritime security. They also endorsed a joint statement on Energy and Climate Change and issued a statement of intent to scale up bilateral co-operation to a global partnership for development co-operation in third countries.

"UK Prime Minister Theresa May visited India from 6-8 November 2016 on her first overseas bilateral visit outside Europe. This reflected the continued importance that UK attaches to its bilateral relationship with India even after UK's decision to leave the European Union.

"Over 30 British business delegates, mostly representing the small and medium enterprise segment accompanied her for the visit. UK PM was also accompanied by Secretary of State for International Trade Dr Liam Fox, MoS for Trade and Investments Greg Hands and National Security Adviser Mark Lyall-Grant. During the visit, the two Prime Ministers agreed to work together on a contemporary and forward-looking global partnership. The two leaders also witnessed thesigning of two MoUs, viz. MoU on co-operation in ease of doing business and MoU on Co-operation in the field of Intellectual Property Rights. Business contracts worth £1.2 billion between British and Indian companies were concluded.

"The Commonwealth Heads of Government meeting in London presented another opportunity for bilateral talks at the apex level between Prime Minister Modi and PM Theresa May. The focus of the visit was on technology and to increase co-operation in trade, investment and finance. It was decided to launch an India-UK Tech Alliance between NASSCOM and Tech UK, establish a UK-India Tech hub, develop UK-India Tech Cluster partnerships, an advanced manufacturing centre in India and collaborate in artificial intelligence and digital healthcare in India's aspirational health districts programme."

The UK has also partnered with India in areas of skill development and is actively involved in the development of smart cities, for examplePune, Indore and Amravati

During the visit of Prime Minister to the UK, a community reception was organised on 13 November 2015 at Wembley Stadium which was attended by over 60,000 persons of Indian origin. The reception was addressed jointly by the Prime Minister along with British Prime Minister David Cameron

Narendra Modi also became the first Indian PM to address the UK Parliament in 2015.

In 2018, Prime Minister was in conversation with a distinguished gathering of the Indian diaspora in a special event titled *'Bharat Ki Baat Sabke Saath'* held at Westminster Central Hall, London on 18 April 2018 and was also telecast live across the globe in countries with Indian diaspora.

France

Source:mea.gov.in

Prime Minister Modi visited France in April 2015 in what was his first visit to a European country. Apart from bilateral meetings with President Francois Hollande and delegation-level talks, the Prime Minister met the parliamentary leaders of France led by Mr Claude Bartolone, President of the French National Assembly and attended business roundtables with CEOs of top French companies. Prime Minister also visited the UNESCO where he launched a special website dedicated to the International Day of Yoga.

Prime Minister Modi visited Paris on 29-30 November 2015 to attend the inaugural leaders' event at the COP-21

Climate Change Summit. He launched the International Solar Alliance jointly with President Hollande in the presence of UN Secretary-General Ban Ki Moon. Along with President Hollande, US President Obama and Microsoft Chairman Bill Gates, he spoke at the event of 'Mission Innovation' for promoting renewable energy. As the Paris Agreement was reached on the conclusion of COP-21, President Hollande praised India's contribution and Prime Minister Modi's personal leadership in reaching the historic agreement.

President Hollande visited India from 24-26 January 2016 as the chief guest of the Republic Day celebration. In a historic first, a French military contingent also marched on Rajpath on the Republic Day and thus France became the first ever foreign country to have been invited to participate in the march.

India and France decided to deepen their bilateral strategic partnership by signing various new agreements during the visit of President Macron to India in March 2018. Both countries concluded a bilateral agreement on 'Exchange and Reciprocal Protection of Classified or Protected Information'. They also issued a 'Joint Strategic Vision of India-France Co-operation in the Indian Ocean Region' to maintain the safety of international sealanes, for countering maritime terrorism and piracy and for building maritime domain awareness. India and France also signed an "agreement for the provision of reciprocal logistics support between their Armed Forces."

India and France have also strengthened co-operation in Defence. India has purchased 36 Rafale jets from France. Smart City projects for Chandigarh, Nagpur and Puducherry have seen active participation from France.

Germany

Modi undertook his first official visit to Germany in April 2015, when India was the Partner Country at the Hannover Messe-2015. At Hannover Messe '15, the world's largest industrial fair, India was awarded the coveted status of Partner Country.

At the inaugural address, India's Prime Minister Modi spoke of "opening many more doors." Hannover Messe 15, has paved the way for new avenues of investment and greater economic engagement between the two nations. The government's flagship programme, #MakeInIndia, was promoted at the industrial fair.

The Make in India Mittelstand (MIIM) programme was launched by the Embassy of India, Berlin in September 2015. It aims at facilitating the entry of German Mittelstand (MSMEs) into India. Currently, 73 German Mittelstand (MSMEs) companies are being facilitated through the MIIM programme for their market entry and investment in India. Out of these 46 companies has progressed well in India investment plan.

Germany is the 7th largest foreign direct investor in India since January 2000. German FDI in India, in 2016, was to the tune of US$ 1.1 billion. Germany's total FDI in India from April 2000 until September 2017 amounted to US$ 10.63 billion. There are more than 1,600 Indo-German collaborations and over 600 Indo-German joint ventures in operation

When Chancellor Markel visited India in 2015, Germany returned a 10th-century relic, a statue of the Hindu goddess Durga in her Mahishasuramardini *avatar*, which had been stolen from India.

Germany and India have decided to co-operate on the

issue of UNSC expansion within the framework of G-4. Both countries consult each other in G-20 on global issues, such as climate change, sustainable development, etc.

Smart City projects for Kochi, Coimbatore and Bhubaneswar have seen active participation from Germany.

Russia

It has been 70 years since India and Russia established formal diplomatic relations. On the occasion of the 70th anniversary, Prime Minister Modi penned an article which was published in Russian newspaper *Rossiyskaya Gazetta* on 31 May 2017.

In his article, Prime Minister Modi highlighted the enduring nature of India- Russia relations:

"India-Russia relations have been the one constant in a world that has changed dramatically since 1947. They have withstood the test of time and grown from strength to strength. The resilience of our relationship is based on the fact that it rests on the principles of equality, trust and mutual benefit. We have adapted our partnership to the different stages of our national development and to the changing realities in the international context. We have been together in times, good and bad."

Prime Minister Modi also highlighted the significant contributions made by Russia in the industrialisation and modernisation of India

"The Soviet Union helped India build its industrial base. The factories at Bokaro and Bhilai, the hydroelectric dam at Bhakra-Nangal and the images of Wing Commander Rakesh Sharma on board the Soyuz T-11 as the first Indian cosmonaut, are etched in the minds of every Indian.

"In the last 70 years, India has developed a large and diversified industrial and technological base. We are among the fastest growing large economies of the world. The potential for India's accelerated growth has never been greater, nor the optimism higher."

Prime Minister Modi also highlighted the need for strong India-Russia relations in the multi-polar world that we live in today:

"At a time of multiple global challenges, our co-operation becomes all the more necessary. There is aloosening of the traditional power balance in the world. New centres of influence and new engines of growth are emerging."

India and Russia relations have seen significant progress under the Modi regime in the fields of commerce, Defence and energy.

As noted by the Ministry of External Affairs:

"During the 17th annual summit held in 2016, India and Russia concluded agreements on thesupply of S-400 air defence systems, construction of frigates under Project 1135.6 and shareholders' agreement on the formation of joint venture to manufacture Ka-226T helicopters in India.

"Indian investments in Russia are estimated to be about US$ 13 billion which include Vankorneft and Taas-Yuryakh Tass fields; Imperial Energy Tomsk; Sakhalin I; Volzhsky Abrasive Works Volgograd and Commercial Indo-Russian Bank. Russian investments in India total about US$ 16 billion, including the acquisition of the ESSAR Group, Kamaz Vectra in Hosur; Shyam Sistema Telecom Ltd, Sberbank and VTB. Earlier, both sides had expressed their desire to raise the level of investments in each other's countries to US $ 15 billion (each way) by 2025. Based upon current figures, it appears that the target will be achieved almost eight years earlier than planned.

Russia is an important partner for India in the area

of peaceful use of nuclear energy. It recognises India as a country with advanced nuclear technology with an impeccable non-proliferation record. In December 2014, Department of Atomic Energy (DAE) and Russia's Rosatom signed the Strategic Vision for strengthening co-operation in peaceful uses of atomic energy between India and Russia. The Kudankulam Nuclear Power Plant (KKNPP) is being built in India with Russian co-operation. KKNPP Units 1 and 2 have already become operational. PM Modi and President Putin jointly dedicated Units 1 & 2 to the nation on separate occasions through videoconferencing. They also initiated the concrete pouring for Units 3 & 4 through video conference on 15 October 2016."

Russia will provide assistance for localisation of nuclear power plants in India. India has been able to balance its ties with Russia given the sanctions on Russia. As the geo-politics of the world changes, Modi government has shown the initiative to maintain good ties with Russia.

One example is the informal summit held between India and Russia at Sochi in May 2018. Both sides agreed to maintain 'strategic equilibrium' and to continue to fight against terrorism.

❐

9
Africa – Mutual Empowerment and Resurgence

The highpoint of India-Africa relations was when India hosted the India-Africa Summit-III which, for the first time enlarged participation from 17 to 54 countries. The summit held in October 2015 unveiled the transformative agenda of mutual resurgence

Speaking at the event, India's Prime Minister Modi placed the rapidly expanding partnership in the context of the interlinked resurgence of India and Africa: "We will raise the level of our support for your vision of a prosperous, integrated and united Africa that is a major partner for the world," he stressed.

The vision document entitled 'Delhi Declaration 2015' and India-Africa Framework for Strategic Co-operation outlined a multi-faceted strategy for dovetailing India growth story with Africa's Agenda 2063 to spur mutual resurgence.

The declaration placed development co-operation at the heart of India-Africa partnership, with India unveiling $10 billion in Lines of Credit for a host of development projects over the next five years and pledging a grant assistance of $600 million. This grant includes an India-Africa Development Fund of $100 million and an India-Africa Health Fund of $10 million.

One-third of the world's humanity lives in India and Africa. Key focus areas of co-operation are food security, maritime security and renewal energy.

With two-thirds of the population of India and Africa under 35 years, human resource development remains the sturdy pillar of India-Africa co-operation. In the last three years alone, nearly 25,000 young Africans have been trained and educated at different institutions in India, forging lasting links between the two emerging regions of the world. The Indian Technical and Economic Co-operation (ITEC) programme exemplifies the transformative power of knowledge-sharing and has acted as a sturdy bridge connecting young Indians and Africans.

India has also made critical contributions in maintaining peace and stability in Africa. India is currently actively involved in four major peacekeeping missions in Africa, which include Democratic Republic of Congo (MONUSCO), South Sudan (UNMISS), Ivory Coast (UNOCI) and Liberia (UNMIL). Put together, India has deployed about 4,500 soldiers on the ground, including the only fully-formed female police unit in Liberia.

The last four years have seen a record number of high-level visits by India, including by PM, President, Vice-President, External Affairs Minister and other ministers. The first-ever meeting of the African Development Bank took place in Ahmedabad in May 2017.

India-Africa relations have the potential to reshape the world order. When 55 countries – India and 54 from Africa — unite with a common vision of bringing development for one-third of humanity using sustainable means, the world cannot help but take notice.

❐

10
India and UN's 2030 Agenda of Sustainable Development

India was among the original members of the United Nations that signed the Declaration by United Nations at Washington on 1 January 1942 and also participated in the historic UN Conference of International Organization at San Francisco from 25 April to 26 June 1945

As a founding member of the United Nations, India strongly supports the purposes and principles of the UN and has made significant contributions to implementing the goals of the Charter, and the evolution of the UN's specialized programs and agencies.

Independent India viewed its membership at the United Nations as an important guarantee for maintaining international peace and security.

India strongly believes that the United Nations and the norms of international relations that it has fostered remain the most efficacious means for tackling today's global challenges. India is steadfast in its efforts to work with the committee of Nations in the spirit of multilateralism to achieve comprehensive and equitable solutions to all problems facing us including development and poverty eradication, climate change, terrorism, piracy, disarmament, peacebuilding and peacekeeping, human rights.

India is partnering with like-minded countries to ensure that the focus of the debate on sustainable development remains on poverty eradication and that RIO principles remain sacrosanct in the global discourse on shaping the post-2015 development agenda. India remains committed to addressing Climate Change through a comprehensive, equitable and balanced outcome based on the principles of equity and common but differentiated responsibilities.

India has been advocating "Zero tolerance" approach to terrorism in all its forms. With the objective of providing a comprehensible legal framework to counter terrorism India took the initiative to pilot a draft Comprehensive Convention on International Terrorism (CCIT) in 1996 and continues to work for its early adoption.

India has a proud history of participation in UN peacekeeping operations dating back to the 1950s, having taken part in as many as 43 peacekeeping operations.

India remains the only State possessing nuclear weapons to call unambiguously for a Nuclear Weapons Convention to ban and eliminate nuclear weapons.

India is today at the forefront of efforts on UN reform, including expansion of the Security Council in both the permanent and nonpermanent categories to reflect contemporary realities.

India is also leading by example when it comes to marching towards the UN's mission of transforming the world by meeting the 2030 Agenda goals. Let us take a look at some of the initiatives taken by India in achieving the 2030 Agenda goals.

Poverty

India has witnessed tremendous growth over the last two decades, the proportion of poor below the poverty line has dropped from 45% to 22% between 1994 and 2012. Close to 133 million Indians have been lifted out of poverty.

Enabling transformation will require investing in all-inclusive solutions to education, financial inclusion, welfare and employment challenges that confront the poor in rural and urban areas. To meet this exponential demand and set the ball rolling for sustaining equitable and inclusive urban development and reducing poverty – the government has launched a series of flagship initiatives – Housing for All, the Atal Mission for Urban Rejuvenation and Transformation (AMRUT), Smart Cities Mission, Digital India, Jan Dhan Yojana and Make in India.

Recent reforms initiated by the Prime Minister have helped increase foreign investment, contributing to a stimulating environment for business; India's ranking in the Global Competitiveness Report improved from 71 in 2014 to 55 in 2015. Policies for the financial and digital inclusion of people living in rural areas have also shown an equalizing effect. The government's initiative to link bank accounts, mobile numbers and national identification numbers (JAM or the Jan Dhan-Aadhaar-Mobile trinity) has contributed to substantial advances in financial inclusion. A flagship initiative for universal banking coverage has also been launched to ensure that every Indian has a bank account, enabling the government to transfer subsidies and other benefits directly to the target beneficiaries and plug leakages in its welfare programs.

Health Water and Sanitation

Life expectancy at birth has doubled since independence, from 33 years in 1947 to 68 years in 2011. The issues of health and well-being are closely related to that of an adequate water supply and functional sanitation systems. India is focused on ensuring access to water and sanitation services to all. Since the launch of Government of India's flagship scheme, the Swachh Bharat Abhiyan (Clean India Mission), more than 12 million toilets have been constructed in rural areas. Equal access to essential health, clean water and sanitation services continue to be a priority for India, which houses one-sixth of the world's population.

There are significant inequalities in access to quality and affordable health services, and a disproportionate burden of communicable and non-communicable disease. The private sector, which provides care to about 70% of the population, is unregulated and poorly integrated into health service delivery systems, despite the lack of infrastructure and human resources in the public sector. Access to life-saving drugs remains a challenge despite India's role as a global pharmacy.

India also faces significant challenges in the provision of quality water, sanitation, solid waste management and drainage. Inequality in access is acute, with more than 90% of urban residents accessing sanitation facilities compared to only 39% in rural India. Additionally, 44% of the population continues to defecate in the open.

The National Health Policy 2017 clearly articulates the government's commitment to reforming the health sector and achieving universal health coverage, not least by proposing an increase in the health budget to 2.5% of GDP. The policy also sets bound targets for disease elimination, reduction of premature and preventable mortality, systems strengthening, as well as improving health services. The government launched Mission Indradhanush in 2015 to rapidly increase immunization coverage. It is also investing significant resources towards ending open defecation by 2019 through the Swachh Bharat program.

The UN also supports the government in achieving the goal of the National Health Policy 2017. UN agencies work with the government to accelerate universal health coverage and strengthen the capacity to provide good and affordable quality health services for all, ending epidemics of key communicable diseases and accelerating the reduction of maternal and newborn deaths, responding to environmental hazards, tackling health security threats from emerging and re-emerging diseases, accelerating sanitation coverage and helping communities to undertake water safety planning to mitigate contamination.

The World Health Organization (WHO) and United Nations Children's Fund (UNICEF) convene the priority area group on health, water, and sanitation. The group includes the Food and Agriculture Organization (FAO), International Organization for Migration (IOM), Joint United Nations Programme on HIV/AIDS (UNAIDS), United Nations Development Programme (UNDP), United Nations Environment Programme (UNEP), United Nations Population Fund (UNFPA), United Nations Entity for Gender Equality and the Empowerment of Women (UN Women), United Nations Office on Drugs and Crime (UNODC), World Food Programme (WFP), and United Nations Human Settlement Programme (UN Habitat).

Gender Equality and Youth Development

Women's economic empowerment is central to the national priority of inclusive economic growth and is critical for the achievement of the Sustainable Development Goals (SDGs). Investing in women's economic empowerment sets a direct path towards gender equality, poverty eradication and inclusive economic growth. The inclusion of women and girls in the economy and the provision of safe working and public spaces must be accompanied by measures to prevent violence against women and girls, and enable them to participate fully in society and contribute to the health and prosperity of their communities.

One in three Indians is a young person, aged 15 to 24 years, and children comprise almost 37% of the country's population. India has the largest youth population in the world. By 2020, the average age of the country will be 29. India's economic growth prospects and achievement of the SDGs will depend largely on their skill, energy and drive to succeed, and on the availability of effective mechanisms to nurture youth leadership, participation and volunteerism. Sixty-five out of the 169 targets for the SDGs reference young people explicitly or implicitly, with a focus on empowerment, participation and well being. Encouraged by the right opportunities, young people can transform the social and economic fortunes of their countries.

Women's economic empowerment is essential to support women in living with dignity in an environment free from violence. The declining child sex ratio (CSR), the practice of gender-biased sex selection, and child marriage all illustrate the extent to which gender discrimination and gender inequality remain significant challenges for India. The incidence of domestic violence against women is also high

Young people can develop the attitudes, agency, skills and behaviour to access and demand information and services to be safe, healthy, to end discrimination and violence, especially against girls, and to help create and sustain a civil society with investments that promote an enabling environment. They must be key partners in shaping new gender inclusive policies and behaviour that can challenge gender stereotypes and norms.

The government has prioritized ending violence against women and introduced special measures to combat trafficking of women and girls, domestic violence, and sexual harassment. It has stepped up efforts to introduce and integrate gender in policy programming. In January 2015, the *Beti Bachao Beti Padhao* (Save Daughter, Educate Daughter) initiative to save and empower the girl child was introduced and is gathering momentum nationally. Skilling and employment programmes for women, along with microfinance services, are reaching underprivileged rural women in distant corners of the country. Legislation to address sexual harassment, domestic violence and unequal remuneration is also being strengthened.

The Government of India's vision to empower young people is articulated in the National Youth Policy 2014. The policy identifies five well-defined objectives and 11 priority areas and suggests policy interventions in each. The priority areas are education, skill development and employment, entrepreneurship, health and healthy lifestyle, sports, promotion of social values, community engagement, participation in politics and governance, youth engagement, inclusion and social justice. The government has undertaken initiatives to enable youth to fully participate in the job market and gain access to employment services. It has launched skill development programs to build the capacity of rural youth, especially those belonging to the below poverty line (BPL) and scheduled caste and tribe categories. Efforts have been made to address health-related issues, physical development, digital inclusion, juvenile crime and delinquency, drug abuse, discrimination against young women, and other youth-specific themes.

A sub-group on gender-based sex selection, comprising UN Women, UNICEF, UNDP and UNFPA, aims to support work around the issue of sex selection and prevention of early marriage.

Powerful advocacy campaigns, such as He For She and 16 Days of Activism against Gender-based Violence (held each year from 25 November to 10 December), have been undertaken. In March 2016, a joint UN communication and advocacy campaign was launched for International Women's Day. The UN partnered with NITI Aayog and My Gov to launch the first-ever Women Transforming India campaign in 2016.

UN Volunteers, along with the Ministry of Youth Affairs and Sports, organised a national consultation to provide inputs into action plans towards the implementation of the National Youth Policy. Young people and technical experts brainstormed on issues related to inclusion, social entrepreneurship, environment and disaster management, gender justice and equality during the consultation.

Skilling, Entrepreneurship and Job Creation

India's economy has grown impressively, with GDP growth rates rising from 5.6% in 2012-13 to 7.6% in 2015-16. The country is poised to grow even faster, with its demographic potential, high investment and savings rates, and allocation of resources for infrastructure. But its high pace of economic growth and notable progress in reducing poverty over the last decade contrasts with the persistent gaps in creating a more inclusive, productive and formal labour market. Investment in skills development will ensure that economic and employment growth is more inclusive. This is especially important in the context of India's demographic transition that has also produced a youth bulge in the working age population.

More than 8 out of every 10 Indian workers are informally employed or work in informal sectors, excluded from employment rights, benefits and social protection. More than half of the non-agricultural working population is absorbed into the informal economy and employment growth remains concentrated in low-productivity sectors, such as construction. Not enough decent and productive jobs have been created. In addition, there are persistent and notable disparities in the labour force participation rates of men and women.

The government has set up the Ministry of Skill Development and Entrepreneurship (MSDE), with an enabling framework to facilitate job creation and entrepreneurship, as well as attract private investment. Steps are also being taken to attract foreign direct investment and catapult manufacturing growth.

The Pradhan Mantri Kaushal Vikas Yojana (Skill India Mission) is MSDE's flagship scheme to enable young Indians to take up industry-relevant skills training and improve their employability.

Several national flagship schemes such as Make in India, Start-up India, Stand-up India (a bank loan program to assist Scheduled Caste, Scheduled Tribe and women borrowers to set up a greenfield enterprise), and Digital India, have been launched to spur the creation of more productive and higher skilled micro, small and medium enterprises, which would accelerate labor demand and job creation. The Atal Innovation Mission endeavorsto promote a culture of innovation and entrepreneurship by providing a platform for the generation and sharing of innovative ideas, alongside an incubator to mentor and support innovators.

The UN priority group on skilling, entrepreneurship and job creation partners with the government to strengthen labor market information systems, extend support for school-to-work transition strategies, as well as help improve the targeting, quality and delivery of employment and skills training program at the state level. It supports the government's job creation and entrepreneurship strategies and program to ensure that young people, women, migrant workers and other marginalized groups are included. Efforts are concentrated in low-income states and districts and the North-East, and sectors including micro, small and medium enterprise (MSME) development, rural labour markets, labour intensive manufacturing, infrastructure development and new sectors such as green industry and affordable housing.

The priority area group is led by the International Labour Organization (ILO) and United Nations Industrial Development Organization (UNIDO), and also includes International Organization for Migration (IOM), United Nations Development Programme (UNDP), United Nations Population Fund (UNFPA), United Nations Entity for Gender Equality and the Empowerment of Women (UN Women), United Nations Human Settlement Programme (UN Habitat), United Nations Educational, Scientific and Cultural Organization (UNESCO) and United Nations Economic and Social Commission for Asia and the Pacific (UNESCAP).

India – United Nations Fund

The India-UN Development Partnership Fund is a dedicated facility within the United Nations Fund for South-South Cooperation established in 2017. It is supported and led by the Government of India, managed by the United Nations Office for South-South Cooperation, and implemented in collaboration with the United Nations system.

South-South cooperation refers to the exchange of resources, technology, and knowledge between developing countries. India has committed $100 million to the Fund over the next decade.

The India-United Nations fund aimed at supporting

sustainable development for low-income nations marked its first anniversary on 8th June, with 22 projects having already been approved in 25 partner countries.

Speaking at the first anniversary of the fund, UN Secretary General, António Guterres commented

"The Fund's focus on supporting people in the least developed countries, small island developing States and landlocked developing States reflects our ambition to reach those that are left furthest behind and to reach them first. India's own development efforts and vision reflected many of the same priorities and aspirations.

India is, for all of us, a very important inspiration"

Peace Keeping

India has also played a remarkable role in United Nations peacekeeping missions in various parts of the world. India is the largest cumulative troop contributor, having provided almost 200,000 troops in nearly 50 of the 71 UN peacekeeping missions over the past six decades, including 13 of the current 16 missions.

International Equality Day

In 2016, Babasaheb Ambedkar's birth anniversary was observed at the United Nations for the first time. India has made a plea to declare April 14 as International Equality Day.

International Equality Day will bring the focus on combating inequalities to achieve Sustainable Development Goals as part of the UN 2030 Agenda.

Over the last 4 years, India has been an inspiration for the world. From fighting poverty, bringing equality and the focus on sustainable development, India is marching ahead to meet the UN's 2030 Agenda Goals.

❐

11
Multi-lateral Summits – Better Governance and Security

In a multipolar world, multi-lateral summits are very important forums to achieve consensus on global issues. Prime Minister Modi has made India's presence felt at all multilateral summits.

Since 2014, Prime Minister Modi has participated in:

- East Asia summits in Myanmar, Kuala Lumpur Laos and Philippines.
- G20 summits in Australia, Turkey, China and Germany.
- SAARC summit in Nepal.
- BRICS summit in Brazil, Russia, China.
- Forum for India-Pacific Island Co-operation (FIPIC) in Fiji.
- NAM summit in Venezuela.
- COP21 summit in France.
- Nuclear Security summit in the US.
- Shanghai Co-operation Organisation in Tajikistan, Russia, Uzbekistan and Kazakhstan.
- Commonwealth summit in the UK.

Here is a list of a few critical outcomes that Modi has managed to achieve in these multi-lateral summits:

1. **Forging a Global Alliance against Black Money –** Curbing black money has now been globally acknowledged as an international problem, helping India preserve billions of dollars which could have been stashed abroad. PM Modi proactively pitched for expanding global co-operation for the return of black money. India's proposed clause on Base Erosion and Profit Sharing Action Plan has been reflected in various G20 declarations.
2. **International Solar Alliance –** In a bid Reduce carbon footprint by leveraging solar power, it was Modi's idea to form a global alliance which to the formation of the International Solar Alliance (ISA). A report by the Observer Research Foundation highlights how Prime Minister Modi has seized the momentum and is driving the agenda to encourage the use of renewable energy—

   "Prime Minister was proactive in finding an ally in the then French President, Francois Hollande, who was also the host of the Paris talks in 2015, and launched the International Solar Alliance (ISA) together with France on the sidelines of the Paris summit — a multilateral body to promote solar growth around the world. ISA's mandate was to bring countries situated within the equatorial tropics together — largely emerging nations — to share best-practices in solar technology and deployment, and provide government-based grants for increased solar adoption.

   With the ISA, PM Modi essentially took a technology largely driven by economics and ensured that he used it to pipe India's commitment to containing greenhouse gas emissions in the face of Western criticism of India's future expected emissions.

In the years since Paris, the world has changed — and PM Modi has seized on the momentum. Obama's departure, and Republican domination in internal US politics, has created a significant lacuna in the climate change momentum globally. Countries have scrambled to find leadership, and have second-guessed each other on baulking out of their emissions-reductions commitments, as Trump already, rather dismissively, has. From Europe too, given that most of the European energy systems have already been built out and that their emissions have plateaued, and the increased fractures in their own internal politics, both at the EU level and at country levels, no clear global leader has emerged on this issue in the face of American vacuum."

3. **Fighting Terror** – In an eloquent vindication of India's concerns over cross-border terror, the G20 summit of the world's most powerful economies in Hamburg culminated in a separate leaders' statement on jointly tackling the scourge of terrorism. In his speech, PM Modi presented an 11-point action agenda for combating terrorism:
   a. Deterrent action by G20 nations against nations supporting terror.
   b. Exchange of national lists of suspected terrorists between G20 countries.
   c. Compulsory joint action is necessary against the named terrorists and their supporters.
   d. Simplify and expedite legal processes, like

extradition for effective co-operation against terrorists.

e. Swift adoption of Comprehensive Convention on International terrorism.
f. Effective implementation of UNSC resolutions and other international processes.
g. Joint efforts by G20 countries on de-radicalisation programmes and exchange of best practices.
h. Effective closure of terror funding through FATF and other means.
i. A Weapons and Explosive Action Task Force (WEATF) should be constituted on the lines of fAtf so that the sources for supplying dangerous weapons to terrorists can be closed.
j. Concrete co-operation is necessary between the G20 nations in the field of cyber security that is focused on terror activities.
k. Formation of the mechanism for national security advisors on counter-terrorism in G20.

India's has successfully used multilateral forums such as BRICS to fight terror and the forces supporting terror. According to a report published by Observer Research Foundation on the Xiamen BRICS Summit in 2017.

"The formulation on the issue of terrorism appearing in the BRICS Declaration on is nothing short of remarkable. The achievement becomes all the more impressive if it is compared with the formulation on the issue that appeared in the Goa Declaration at the end of the 8th BRICS Summit on 16 October

2016. In the run-up to the last summit, Modi had severely chastised Pakistan for its terrorist activities against India and in other parts of the world and termed it as the "mothership of terrorism". China (and Russia) had fought hard to keep any reference to cross-border terrorism or to Pakistan-based terrorist groups out of the summit declaration. In fact, China mentioned terrorism along with natural and manmade disasters in its plenary statement. Russia did not make any reference to the 'T' word in its statement. In comparison, the hard-hitting language against terrorism and specific mention of Pak-based terrorist groups like Lashkar-e-Taiba (LeT), Jaish-e-Mohammad (JeM) and others like Taliban, Haqqani Network etc., is nothing but exceptional."

4. **Good Governance –** At the World Government Summit held in Dubai, Prime Minister Modi advocated the use of technology to provide better services to citizens. Technology provides the scale needed to provide maximum governance with a minimum government. India's use of technology, such as Aadhar, is being studied and appreciated the world over.
5. **World Economic Forum –** Narendra Modi became the first Indian Prime Minister to deliver a keynote address at the World Economic Forum in Davos. In his speech, Prime Minister Narendra highlighted climate change, terrorism and the backlash against globalisation are the three most significant challenges facing the

world today and shared India's vision for a shared, interconnected world.

India's presence at multi-lateral summits is now being felt. Our Prime Minister is one of the most sought-after and heard leaders at these summits. The world largest democracy and fastest growing economy is now being heard worldwide.

❐

12
Heal the World – International Yoga Day

Speaking at the United Nations General Assembly (UNGA) in September 2014, Prime Minister Modi suggested:

"Yoga is an invaluable gift of India's ancient tradition. It embodies the unity of mind and body; thought and action; restraint and fulfilment; harmony between man and Nature; a holistic approach to health and well-being. It is not about exercise but to discover the sense of oneness with yourself, the world and Nature. By changing our lifestyle and creating consciousness, it can help in our well-being. Let us work towards adopting an International Yoga Day."

—Narendra Modi

Following this initial proposal, the UNGA held informal consultations on the draft resolution entitled 'International Day of Yoga', on 14 October 2014.

When, on 11 December 2014, India introduced the draft resolution on International Yoga Day to be celebrated on 21st June, it received support from 177 member nations. It was for the first time in the history of the United Nations that 177 member nations collectively decided to co-sponsor a resolution. India's resolution was adopted without a vote and since then, 21 June is being celebrated as International

Yoga Day globally.

When proposing 21 June as the date, Modi said that the date was the longest day of the year in the Northern Hemisphere (shortest in the Southern Hemisphere), having special significance in many parts of the world.

Source: http://yoga.ayush.gov.in

The summer solstice marks the transition to *Dakshinayana*. The first full moon after summer solstice is known as *Guru Poornima*. Shiva, the first yogi (Adi Yogi), is said to have begun imparting the knowledge of yoga to the rest of mankind on this dayand became the first guru (Adi Guru). Dakshinayana is also considered the time when there is a natural support for those pursuing spiritual practices.

The first Yoga Day was celebrated on 21 June 2015. In India, 35,985 people from 84 nations came together to create a *Guinness World Record*. In San Francisco, 5,000 participants gathered in the Marina Green Park to practice yoga.

In 2016, India organised a special event at the United

Nations on International Yoga Day. A special event titled 'Conversation with Yoga Masters – Yoga for the Achievement of Sustainable Development Goals (SDGs)' was the highlight of the event.

Since then, every year, millions across the world have followed the path of the Adi Yogi and celebrated Yoga Day and India could realise the dream of Swami Vivekananda — of being a *vishwa guru*.

❐

13
International Solar Alliance

Indian culture and way of life have always revered the environment. Mountains, rivers, trees, animals and Nature have held a special place for Indians.

Indian culture subscribes to the belief that we have the right to take from the environment only that which we need and can be naturally replenished. Exploiting Nature for man's greed has never been acceptable in India.

Source:http://isolaralliance.org

It is, therefore no surprise that it was an Indian Prime Minister who dreamt of an International Solar Alliance. The idea of an International Solar Alliance was first suggested by Prime Minister Modi in a speech to the Indian diaspora at the Wembley Stadium in November 2015. In his speech, Prime Minister called all the countries that lie completely or partly between the Tropic of Cancer and Tropic of Capricorn to come together and form an alliance which would harness solar energy. Prime Minister Modi referred to these countries as 'sunshine countries' or *suryaputras* (sons of the Sun).

The purpose of the International Solar Alliance was to use solar energy as a cleaner and sustainable alternative to fossil fuels. The International Solar Alliance was launched by Prime Minister Modi at the India-African summit and at the meeting of member countries ahead of the 2015 United Nations Climate Change Conference at Paris in November 2015

The framework agreement of the International Solar Alliance opened for signatures in Marrakech, Morocco in November 2016, and 121 countries have joined.

In January 2016, Narendra Modi and the then French President François Hollande laid the foundation stone of the ISA headquarters and inaugurated the interim Secretariat at the National Institute of Solar Energy (NISE) in Gwalpahari, Gurugram, India.

India has provided five acres of land on the NISE campus for its future headquarters; it also has contributed 1.75 billion (US$27 million) to the fund to build a campus and for meeting expenditure for the first five years.

The launching of such an alliance in Paris also sends a strong signal to the global communities about the sincerity of the developing nations towards their concern about climate change and to switch to a low-carbon growth path.

India has pledged a target of installing 100GW by 2022 and reduction in emission intensity by 33–35 per cent by 2030 to let solar energy reach the most unconnected villages and communities and also towards creating a clean planet. India's pledge at the Paris summitoffered to bring 40 per cent of its electricity generation capacity (not actual production) from non-fossil sources (renewable, large hydro and nuclear) by 2030, is based on world co-operation.

ISA has also partnered with the World Bank and developed an online tool that displays the potential for solar energy in any part of the world. This tool will help in the identification of sites for solar farms.

India leveraged her diplomatic engagements around the world to mobilise support for the International Solar Alliance. This will scale up the production of solar energy, thereby providing a clean source of energy to millions of Indians.

Development of 121 solar projects was approved at the founding conference of ISA in March 2018.

International Solar Alliance will also provide technological and financial support for enhanced production of renewable energy, which will reduce pollution and improve public health. India-led ISA is a ray of hope for many countries which seek energy security while addressing issues of pollution and global warming at the same time.

One more time, Narendra Modi has realised Swami Vivekananda's dream of India emerging as a *vishwa guru.*

❐

14
Securing Indians Globally

Foreign policy work is commonly associated with glitzy high-level diplomatic summits, where world leaders make speeches and sign documents, be it peace treaties or trade agreements, all under the glare of a thousand flashbulbs. And while these are, of course, important and do aim to deliver good to the public, often the spotlight tends to blight out those in whose name all this is done: the citizen.

Yet, it is the citizen and theirwelfare that should lie at the core of any nation's foreign policy; and securing the citizen's interests at home and abroad must be the most important yardstick with which to measure the success of any diplomatic effort. It in this context that India's Minister for External Affairs, Sushma Swaraj has proved herself to be a class apart.

The External Affairs Minister, Sushma Swaraj has been winning hearts since the time she took over, by helping many Indians in times of trouble.

Swaraj's presence online is also a good example of how citizens and the government can directly connect with each other. Using Twitter, her team has helped several Indians living abroad in times of crises.

From reuniting families to helping citizens recover their passport and travel home safe, every request for help, whether small or big, gets the minister's attention.

Sushma's efforts have earned her the monikers such as 'the Supermom of the State', 'The Twitter queen', 'The common Tweeple's Leader'. Not only that, the *Foreign Policy* magazine has included her in the list "for fashioning a novel brand of Twitter diplomacy" and her inclusion in the list of 100 Global Thinkers.

Sushma Swaraj is known for her humanitarian work and rapid response to any user in need of medical visas for treatment in India. Swaraj has been adopting a humanitarian approach in granting visas to Pakistani nationals on medical grounds, despite the strain in ties between the two sides over a host of sticky issues, including cross-border terrorism.

In December 2017, Sushma Swaraj asked for a report from India's Consul General in Chicago about an attack on a 30-year-old Indian national in the United States, Mohammad Akbar. Sushma Swaraj tweeted, "I have asked for a report from our Consul General in Chicago."

Mohammad Akbar was seriously injured in the shooting on December 6 that happened near the Albany Park neighbourhood in Chicago, according to a report by PTI. Mohammad was admitted in a serious condition at Illinois Masonic Medical Centre after he was shot in the cheek. In another tweet, Swaraj informed that she had sought details from the Uttar Pradesh government on reports that a number of foreign tourists were beaten up in Mirzapur.

The other instance is India's humanitarian assistance to the Republic of Yemen. The Government of India provided medical assistance worth about US$ one million to the Republic of Yemen in response to a request from the Yemeni government.

As a part of its commitment to provide humanitarian

assistance to Yemen, India has been a member of the 'Friends of Yemen' Group. India had earlier extended medical assistance to Yemen in April 2015. Additionally, India provided food assistance in the form of rice and wheat, each worth of US$ 2 million in August 2012 and March 2013 respectively.

In response to the humanitarian crisis being faced on account of the large influx of refugees into Bangladesh, Government of India has decided to extend assistance to Bangladesh under Operation Insaniyat. The relief material consists of items required urgently by the affected people, namely rice, pulses, sugar, salt, cooking oil, tea, ready-to-eat noodles, biscuits, mosquito nets, etc.

India has always responded readily and swiftly to any crisis in Bangladesh, in keeping with the close ties of friendship between the peoples of India and Bangladesh. India stands ready to provide any assistance required by Government of Bangladesh in this hour of need.

Swaraj is not an exception on Twitter. When it comes to using social media, this government has been unlike any in India in its efforts to turn it into a tool of governance, transparency, communication and, not to forget, public relations. India's External Affairs Minister navigates the treacherous waters of social media with a rare clarity of purpose, warmth and sense of direction. Sushma Swaraj is a regular on Twitter, responding to various requests for help from NRIs. From reuniting families to helping citizens recover their passport and travel home safe, every request for help, whether small or big, get her personal attention.

The Foreign Minister helped out, with clear instructions to the Indian embassy in the US, to issue an urgent visa to an American citizen of Indian origin whose father has died in India. The plea came from Sarita Takru in Karnal: "Sushma

Swaraj, lost my husband yesterday. My only child Abhai Kaul (American) citizen can't get Indian visa before Thursday." And after several quick exchanges, the distressed woman was informed: "Our embassy contacted your son. He should submit an application and collect visa from our consulate in Chicago."

Aliya Harir, part of a delegation of young Pakistani women, was worried about their safe return in the wake of India's surgical strikes against terrorist bases across the Line of Control at the end of September. In the middle of mounting tension, Swaraj spread a quintessentially South Asian view of motherhood: "I was concerned about your well-being because daughters belong to us all." It was an extraordinary intervention that could only have come from a woman.

At the annual conference held by the Ministry of External Affairs, it was reported that 90,000 Indians have been recused in the last four years.

Some of the more known cases are:

Geeta, a deaf and dumb girl from India, who wandered into Pakistan more than 15 years ago was brought back home. Sushma Swaraj not only got Geeta home but is also working hard to locate her parents.

Judith D'souza was working with the Aga Khan Foundation as a senior technical advisor in Kabul. She was kidnapped on 9 June 2016 and was rescued by India in July.

Sushma Swaraj
@SushmaSwaraj

Judith D'Souza is with us - safe and in good spirits. She will reach her Motherland at the earliest. Vande Mataram. twitter.com/SushmaSwaraj/s...

08:54 - 23 Jul 2016

2,309 1,324 people are talking about this

Source: mea.gov.in

From Yemen, Father Tom Uzhunnalil was rescued after more than a year in captivity. Father Tom was taken hostage in March 2016 after an attack on his home. With co-operation from Oman, India has managed to bring home Father Tom.

Father Alexis Prem Kumar, who was abducted in Afghanistan, was also rescued.

Gurpreet, a mother of an eight-year old girl posted a video on the internet in which she claimed that she was tricked by her husband's family to move to Germany and was now confined to a refugee camp. External Affairs Minister, Sushma Swaraj quickly swung into action and ensured a safe return for Gurpreet and her daughter.

Indian passport is today the best security insurance for an Indian when abroad. The External Affairs Ministry under Sushma Swaraj has always put Indian's first. Here are a few examples of large-scale evacuations facilitated by India:

- 1,100 Indians evacuated from Ukraine in 2014.
- 7,200 Indians evacuated from Iraq.
- 3,750 Indians evacuated from Libya.
- 4,748 Indians evacuated from Yemen.
- 157 Indians evacuated from South Sudan.

Indian help is no longer limited to Indians. Nearly 1962 foreign nationals from 48 countries were rescued by India from Yemen in 2015. Operation Maitri was the largest ever disaster-relief assistance provided by India to Nepal in 2015.

'Operation Insaniyat' provided food relief to refugees in Bangladesh. 'Operation Neer' provided drinking water to the Maldives.

Using *'kut-niti'* (diplomacy) for *'lok-niti'* (welfare of citizens) has been the hallmark of the External Affairs Ministry under Sushma Swaraj.

❒

15

Indian Diaspora – Our Cultural Ambassadors

The Indian diaspora abroad has a long history. Hundreds of years ago, Indian traders set up trading posts in the Persian Gulf and Southeast Asia. When India was part of the British Empire, tens of thousands of Indian citizens were recruited by the British to work on plantations in colonies all around the world, from Fiji to Mauritius, from South Africa to the Caribbean basin.

There is an Indian diaspora in 130 countries around the world, with a total population of more than 27 million. Today, immigrants from India have economic and political clout far beyond Mauritius, Fiji and Guyana. In addition to the 3.1 Indian immigrants living in the United States, there are 1.5 million in the United Kingdom; 1 million in Canada; 1.2 million in South Africa and 6 million in the Middle East.

Members of the Indian diaspora have high incomes, are well educated, play a significant role in the scientific and technological life of the countries in which they live and wield political and social influence.

A distinctive feature of Prime Minister Modi's foreign policy is his direct call to the Indian diaspora abroad. Every appearance he has made since he came to office – at Wembley

Stadium in London, Madison Square Garden in New York and Dubai International Cricket Stadium; in Toronto, Kuala Lumpur, Paris and Seychelles – has turned into a show, a kind of 'Modi-mania', with thousands of people chanting the Indian leader's name.

During his three years in office, PM Modi has proactively reached out to the Indian diaspora in different countries, including US, Australia, UK, the Gulf and Israel.

He has lavished praise on the Indian diaspora for their remarkable achievements, while also reminding them of their roots. Inaugurating the 14th Pravasi Bharatiya Divas (Overseas Indian Day) in Bengaluru in January 2017, Modi said, "There are over 30 million overseas Indians living abroad…their footprints are all over the world…Indians abroad are valued not for their strength in numbers …they are respected for their contributions to India and the societies where they live. In foreign lands and communities across the globe, the Indian diaspora represents for their values. They are hardworking, law abiding and peace loving, and are role models for other communities."

The Modi government wants to leverage the Indian diaspora as a foreign policy tool. While addressing the diaspora in the Netherlands, the PM stated, "Every Indian abroad is a diplomat." But the Prime Minister wants the diaspora not just to represent India's interests overseas, but also to contribute to India's economic development by investing back home and contributing to development schemes undertaken by the government

For the first time, India's Foreign Minister is focusing on Indian affairs overseas. The government has decided on a single identity card to make it easier for the diaspora to connect with the homeland, secure lifelong Indian visas, avoid checks at local police stations during visits and own land. India also allowed visitors from 43 countries, including the United States, Australia and Fiji, to receive visas upon arrival, replacing the previous process, which took weeks.

Now many say they feel closer to India, "Many of us in the diaspora who felt like a severed entity felt reconnected to the Indian mothership when Narendra Modi reached out and embraced us the way he did in New York," said Saureen Shah, a 33-year-old engineer and Indian-American citizen in San Francisco who came to India to work for Modi's election campaign last year. "It was like pressing the restart button in our relationship with India."

If Atal Bihari Vajpayee laid the foundation for reimaging India's ties with the diaspora at the turn of the millennium, Modi has made it a key area of national priority. For Modi, the diaspora is an 'asset' rather than a 'liability' and India's intellectual power beyond borders is 'brain gain' and not 'brain drain'.

Before Modi, Indian embassies abroad would organise formal receptions with a few dozen prominent Indians when Prime Ministers visited. But Modi prefers to reach out to larger numbers cutting across age, occupation and income.

In New York, in September 2014, hundreds of Indians lined up on the streets to catch a glimpse of Modi, shake hands and take selfies with him.

"You play a key role in shaping a positive image of India not just in America but also around the world," Modi told a rapturous crowd of more than 22,000 Indians, cheering and chanting at Madison Square Garden. About 20 members of Congress attended the event, which pleased many in Modi's political party here because they hoped it would help create politically assertive Indian communities abroad.

His speech, when it came, did not disappoint. Casting himself as a man of humble origins with "the intention to do big things for small people," he vowed to promote Indian economic growth, clean up the polluted Ganges river and improve the lot of the country's poor and disadvantaged. He promised to make it easier for those of Indian descent to obtain visasso that members of the Indian diaspora might bring their talents back to the homeland.

Prime Minister Modi paid an official visit to the Republic of Indonesia (May 29-31) and Republic of Singapore (May 31-June 2) at the invitation of H.E. Mr. Joko Widodo, President of the Republic of Indonesia and H.E. Mr. Lee Hsien Loong, Prime Minister of Singapore respectively.

After his arrival, PM Modi was given a warm welcome by the Indian community at The Ritz Carlton in Jakarta.

"You represent thousands of years of the shared culture and civilisation, geography and history, aspiration and achievements of the great sons and daughters of India and Myanmar," the Prime Minister said, addressing the gathering of the Indian community in Yangon, Myanmar, 6 September 2017.

Source: @narendramodi

The Prime Minister, on 30th May, addressed the Indian community in Jakarta. The event was attended by around 3,000 members of the Indian diaspora in Indonesia.

He spoke of the special ties between India and Indonesiaand recalled the Republic Day celebrations in New Delhi earlier this year, where leaders from 10 ASEAN nations, including Indonesiawere present. He said the members of the Indian diaspora in Indonesia are proud citizens of Indonesia, but wish to remain connected with their Indian roots as well.

He spoke of FDI, the openness of the Indian economy, ease of doing business and competitiveness of the Indian economy.

During his speech, Modi also touched on the "close and ancient relations" between Indonesia and India, especially as maritime neighbours.

He said both countries are proud of their democratic ethos and diversity. He gave examples, such as the Bali-Jatra, and similarities in cuisine and language to highlight the close cultural links between the two countries

Both India and Indonesia have a sensitive outlook when it comes to helping those in need, the Prime Minister asserted. He said that India does not see the colour of anyone's passport and helps all fellow humans who require any assistance. He said India and Indonesia do not just rhyme in their names, but share a common rhythm in their culture, traditions and democratic values.

Urging the Indian community in Indonesia to visit India once again to "see for themselves the things that are happening in India," he also mentioned that the Indian government is working to grant Indonesian tourists free 30-day visas.

On 18 April 2018 Prime Minister Modi addressed the Indian diaspora in Sweden's Stockholm University.

Source:@narendramodi

During the interaction with the Indian diaspora in Sweden, PM Modi said that after four years of efforts, the world today sees India as a dependable partner. He highlighted several achievements of the Indian government which are helping alleviation of poverty, increase in health care and strengthen ease of doing business through *'sabka sath, sabka vikas'*.

Highlighting the importance of non-resident Indians in the development story of the nation, he invited the diaspora to invest in India. "Emerging new India is a pool for investment opportunity for the diaspora. To trade, innovate and invest, come to India."

He even congratulated them for keeping alive the soul of India and Indian values even after living outside India and appreciated how they have carved out a niche for themselves through innovative skills, professional attitude, cultural integration and Indian values.

After many years the relationship between India and the countries of the Gulf region has developed a strong bond. On 11 February 2018 PM addressed nearly 3.3 million strong Indian diaspora at the Dubai Opera House.

He talked about corruption-free, development-centric governance. He officially launched the foundation stone-laying ceremony for the first Hindu temple in the capital of the UAE, home to over three million people of Indian origin.

Moving further to the Netherlands which has the second largest Indian diaspora in entire Europe.

Modi mostly focused on his government's efforts aimed at women's empowerment as he talked about the endeavour to ensure progress and modernisation of India.

He highlighted the diversity existing in India and said it was the country's 'speciality' which puzzled people in other parts of the world.

He mentioned the various initiatives taken by his government in sectors like banking, energy and digitalisation and talked about the progress being made in areas like space, healthcare and sanitation.

Undertaking a 'ground-breaking' visit, Narendra Modi became the first-ever Indian Prime Minister to step on Israeli soil on 4 July 2017.

Modi addressed a gathering of about 5,000 Israelis of Indian origin at a convention centre in Tel Aviv.

In his speech, Modi recalled several Jewish Indians who had served in India, including General J.F.R. Jacob and hundreds of Indians who worked to "make the desert bloom" in Israel for farming jobs.

The PM recounted the government's achievements, including the introduction of GST unified tax, housing subsidies and the use of 'neem-coated' fertilisers. He also promised the diaspora faster facilitation of PIO and OCI cards, as well as visas, and the setting up of an Indian cultural centre in Israel 'very soon'.

For the first time, an Indian Prime Minister has visited the East African nation in 34 years. Addressing the Indian diaspora of around 11,000 people in South Africa's Johannesburg, Modi said, "It was in South Africa that Mahatma Gandhi conceptualised his politics. This is the birthplace of *satyagraha*. Every non-resident Indian is now a diplomat or a cultural ambassador for India. Their organised and collective might have often influenced their governments to see and treat India differently.

❐

16
Vishwa Guru Bharat

There is little doubt that foreign policy under the Narendra Modi government has undergone a complete transformation. India used to be a reluctant participant in the geopolitics of Asia and the world; India now has an active and innovative foreign policy.

The energy and personality of Prime Minister Narendra Modi have played a pivotal role in this transformation. He has put neighbours first, acted East, linked West Asia, is no longer shy about Israel, has built momentum with Europe and rejuvenated ties with the US.

Prime Minister's actions have been guided by one purpose – diplomacy for the development of India. Economic diplomacy and leveraging the Indian diaspora as cultural ambassadors have been the foundational elements of Modi's foreign policy.

Indian passport is no longer a liability but a security shield for any Indian. Every Indian knows that when in need, the Narendra Modi government will come to his or her rescue.

India under Modi has also lived up to Swami Vivekananda's dream of being a *vishwa guru*. International Yoga Day, International Solar Alliance, India-Africa summits are good examples where India demonstrated leadership at a global level.

A multi-polar world today is in search of a new paradigm.

Speaking at the Shangri-La Dialogue, Prime Narendra Modi outlined a 5S paradigm:

1. *Sammaan*, i.e. respect
2. *Samvaad*, i.e. dialogue
3. *Sahayog*, i.e. co-operation
4. *Shanti*, i.e. Peace
5. *Samruddhi*, i.e. Prosperity

India has treated every country with *Samaan* (respect) irrespective of the size of their economy. India seeks to engage the world on the principle of mutual respect. *Samvaad* or dialogue continues at bilateral or multilateral forums. India does not want to compete with China or Japan for dominance in the region but to work with them for the greater good of Asia. Peace and prosperity for all lies at the soul of India's foreign policy. From Chankya to Narendra Modi, India has never once deviated from this goal.

Modi's view of a multi-polar world is where:

- There exists mutual respect and not just tolerance.
- Dialogue takes precedence over disputes.
- There is more co-operation between countries and less competition.
- Peace in lieu of wars.
- Prosperity for all, rather than a few.

India's foreign policy over the last four years reminds us of the *shloka* from *Maha Upanishad*:

अयं बन्धुरयं नेति गणना लघुचेतसाम्।
उदारचरितानां तु वसुधैव कुटुम्बकम्॥

One is a relative, the other a stranger,
say the small minded.
The entire world is a family, live the magnanimous.

—Maha Upanishad 4.71

□□□